ROOTED
in JESUS:
Healing
Generational
Defects

ROOTED in JESUS:
Healing Generational Defects

Patricia A. McLaughlin

Queenship
PUBLISHING COMPANY
P.O. Box 220 • Goleta, CA 93116
(800) 647-9882 • (805) 692-0043 • Fax: (805) 967-5133

About the cover.

"And he shall be as a tree that is planted by the waters, that spreadeth out its roots towards moisture: and it shall not fear when the heat cometh. And the leaf thereof shall be green, and in the time of drought it shall not be solicitous, neither shall it cease at any time to bring forth fruit."
(Jer 17:8-9)

Front cover photograph by *Rex McLaughlin*.
Back cover photograph by *Stephen Ryan Photographics*.

All scriptural quotes are from The Jerusalem Bible, unless noted otherwise.

Excerpts from THE JERUSALEM BIBLE, copyright (c) 1966 by Darton, Longman & Todd, Ltd. and Doubleday, a division of Bantam Doubleday Dell Publishing Group, Inc. Reprinted by Permission.

Those noted are from The New American Bible.

Library of Congress Number # 02-141055

Published by:
    Queenship Publishing
    P.O. Box 220
    Goleta, CA 93116
    (800) 647-9882 • (805) 692-0043 • Fax: (805) 967-5133
    http://www.queenship.org

Printed in the United States of America

ISBN: 1-57918-190-2

CONTENTS

DEDICATED WITH
LOVE, BLESSINGS, AND GRATITUDE TO:

My Heavenly Father, for showering his blessings upon all
generations of my family tree: past, present and future;
My husband, Rex, for his constant love, faithfulness, and support;
Our ancestors, for their gift of life and all they have taught me:
McLaughlin, Mealey, Sweeney, Supry, New, Egan, Conlon, Fitzgerald,
Murtagh, Loveland, Fritz, Culp, Bolinger, Brennan, Bryant, & those
not yet discovered;   Our family branches: Hauck, Naia, Parker, and theirs;
Our living family tree, for the blessings and the happiness they bring to my life:
Anne Theresa, Christopher Michael, Thomas Joseph, Diane Louise,
John Patrick, Florence Celeste, Joseph James, Patrick Dennis, Jennifer Lynne,
Ambia Therese, Megan Kelly, Duane Michael, Cayla Loren,
Florence Ann, Sean Thomas, Joseph James, Jr., Bridgit Celine;
With special blessings on those to follow.

"You must
live your
whole life
according
to the Christ
you have
received –
J E S U S the LORD.
You must be rooted in him and built on him and
held firm by the faith you have been taught,
and full of thanksgiving." (Col 2:6-7)

Anne Theresa McLaughlin
June 25, 1956 - December 14, 2001
Always God's Child
Always Loved

ACKNOWLEDGMENTS

This book could not have been written without the help of many special people. I extend my heartfelt gratitude to all who have been involved in my family's healing; to my family and friends for their love and prayers; to Claire Schaeffer for her enthusiasm and encouragement; to Father Michael Barry, SS.CC. for his gifts of healing and friendship; Father John H. Hampsch, C.M.F. for his prayers and shared wisdom; to Doctor Kenneth McAll for the gift of his teachings; to Lori Mountain, R.N. for her faith and prayers; and to the Association of Christian Therapists, my loving extended family.

There is a season for everything,
a time for every occupation under heaven....
A time for tears, a time for laughter;
a time for mourning, a time for dancing. (Eccl 3:14)

You are the heirs of the prophets, the heirs of
the covenant God made with our ancestors when
he told Abraham, "In your offspring all the families
of the earth shall be blessed."   (Acts 3:25)

A blessing on the man who puts his trust in Yahweh,
with Yahweh for his hope.
He is like a tree by the waterside
That thrusts its roots to the stream:
When the heat comes it feels no alarm,
Its foliage stays green;
It has no worries in a year of drought,
And never ceases to bear fruit. (Jer 17:8-9)

A NOTE TO THE READER

Popular books by child guidance experts, sociologists, psychologists, and others address contemporary family concerns. This book addresses the same concerns, but with the focus on problems that are rooted in generational issues within the family. Generational healing has, as its primary objective, the healing of the living family through prayers for reconciliation with past generations. Prayer is directed at the inherited effects of generational sin, which includes any attitudes, behaviors, diseases, and weaknesses that have contaminated the family line. Generational healing touches the living, while asking God to bring deceased family members into the full presence of his peace and glory. It also provides an inheritance of blessings for future generations.

Love is the basic teaching of Jesus and sometimes those most difficult to love are the people within our own families. *Rooted in Jesus* addresses your need for healing personal and familial relationships. It also considers the possibility of inherited defects, while stressing the positive inheritance you received from your ancestors.

Everyone can pray to Jesus for healing because the Son of God uses the prayers and touch of ordinary people to accomplish his healing. Jesus, who loves us and wants to walk with us, is the ultimate healer of body, mind, and spirit. In *The Jesus Walk: The Road to Healing Body and Soul*, I provided a model for conventional healing prayer, which can result in a change of heart that leads to deeper healing.

Complex problems such as addiction, psychological instability, and deep-seated illnesses often require a more systematic approach. For afflictions that do not respond to ordinary prayers for healing, the need for generational healing may be indicated. This approach often leads to layers of healing.

The power of Jesus to heal across generations is vital for families in today's troubled world. This book will be your guide through the discernment process that directs your prayers for family healing. It is founded on Christ's love for his people and his willingness to heal.

An investigation of the past may uncover failings and weaknesses in our ancestors, but we might find much to celebrate in the positive traits and attitudes that they passed down through the generations. Even negative traits can result in positive effects when we understand the causes of the negativity and view our ancestors with Christ's love. As we develop "Jesus hearts"—hearts of love and compassion—we learn to redirect our energies more positively towards family peace and healing. Through prayers concentrated on forgiveness and healing of ancestral relationships, walls of unforgiveness are dismantled and old grudges and biases are abandoned. Family tree healing is usually centered on the celebration of the Eucharist. It is important to note, however, that God is not limited by our method of prayer. Sincere prayers are always heard and answered by him in a loving way.

Rooted in Jesus emphasizes the need to redeem the past and sanctify the present and the future. It also addresses the needs of families to grow strong, unified, and morally healthy. It encourages attitudes of thanksgiving and appreciation for the blessings received from forebears. Above all, it celebrates peace and healing within families.

Past, present, and future generations of your family can benefit from your prayers for generational healing. Your present family can be set free from any ties to the past which may be responsible for mental, physical, and emotional illness passed down the family line from previous generations. Just as dry bones came to life when Yahweh breathed upon them (Ez 37:1-14), God will breathe new life into the dry bones of your broken ancestors, making them come alive for you as real, suffering people in need of healing. When you heal the present, you impact the future.

The success of family healing relies upon the mercy of God but it also depends upon cooperation with his grace and the willingness to make life changes. The destructive patterns of addictions, bad habits, and negative attitudes must be replaced with positive life-giving behavior, for without change healing may be blocked. Adherence to such patterns also results in a negative legacy for future generations of your family.

Through generational healing, Jesus restores your family's

health and creates an environment in which family members can grow strong. *Rooted in Jesus* provides the tools, guidance, and inspiration to help your preparation for a family tree healing. This is your opportunity to write a new chapter for your living family, while ensuring a brighter, more peaceful prospect for generations yet to come.

On the 1996 World Day of Peace, Pope John Paul II stressed family peace, urging, "Let us give children a future of peace." Healing divisions and brokenness within families is a giant step towards fostering peace in the world. Parents who model peace bless their children and offer a troubled world new hope for the future.

May peace and blessings be the rich inheritance you pass down to future generations of your family.

Patricia A. McLaughlin

Feast of All Souls, 2001

1. THE GIFT OF FAMILY

*"I came that you might have life
and have it to the full."* (Jn 10:1)

You were created as part of a family, and family is one of the greatest gifts God has given to us. In his wisdom, he created us with basic needs, and then provided a social structure to provide for those needs. He also gave us free will, conscience, intelligence, and memory. Free will allows us to get into trouble, while conscience attempts to direct our choices and correct our sinful inclinations. When we explore our roots in search of deep healing for our families, intelligence and memory come to our aid.

In years past, family was the backbone of the community. Today, experts in many fields agree that the traditional family structure is an endangered species. Marriages are failing at an alarming rate. The weakening of marriage, combined with economic and societal changes, is contributing to the moral and mechanical breakdown of the family. Meanwhile, a strong interest in genealogical research is prompting many to research their family histories. Research into family history can reveal destructive patterns that may have undermined family cohesiveness.

Genealogical research is more than a nostalgic pastime. Recent advances in the field of genetics emphasize the importance of assessing your family's predisposition to inherited diseases. With knowledge of your family's medical history, some diseases can be prevented or minimized through medical intervention and lifestyle changes.[1] Many family therapists utilize genograms (family tree charts with notations describing relationships and characteristics) to determine causes and cure of emotional problems.

While the practical benefits of genealogy are undeniable, the healing of generations through prayer yields multiple rewards. With knowledge gained from your family history research, you can discern the root causes of family defects. Family unity and reconciliation, as well as spiritual, physical, and emotional healing can result from your informed prayers. You will also gain a deeper appreciation of your ancestors and the gifts you have inherited.

Consider your research a work of love. By preserving your family's history and traditions, you are creating a unique gift that only you can give. Your story will be treasured by future generations, who may be inspired to embrace old family values and traditions.

ROOTEDNESS

When I first began to research my family's history, I had no idea what I would find. I scarcely knew where to begin my search, but my motivation was strong because I perceived a deep need for family healing. Healing of my daughter's mental illness was my primary concern. In 1979, at the age of twenty-two, she was diagnosed with chronic schizophrenia. Even though I had been gifted with a healing ministry, I did not know how to help her. When I learned about generational healing a few years later, I felt renewed hope for her recovery.

On a personal level, I knew so little about my forebears, I felt a part of me was missing. When I finally located the missing component, I recognized it immediately and was able to name it. Rootedness, the sense of family that goes beyond father, mother, and siblings, had been lacking in my childhood.

As an only child, I was raised within the narrowest family boundaries. During my early years, chronic illness pretty much isolated me from my peers and caused me to miss many ordinary childhood experiences. Then, when I was nine, my parents and I moved from Illinois to Arizona. In the ensuing years, my connection with the relatives I had known in Illinois was severed and they became only a memory.

When I researched my family's history, God gave me a new appreciation of my ancestors. He also supplied insights to guide my prayers of healing for past, present, and future generations of our family. Generational healing is not a quick, one-time cure for every family ill. Rather it is a form of personal healing which requires prayer, effort, and patience with the process. Furthermore, it does not relieve your ongoing responsibility to nurture family relationships. Generational prayer is an aid to healing but is not a substitute for your other family obligations.

The search for family ties can take you on a journey of understanding and discernment. The discoveries you make will give you a new perception of who you are, as well as a feeling of rootedness and connection with your ancestors. Honoring your family history enriches your life story.

TROUBLE IN THE GARDEN

Original sin, which we inherit along with our human nature, is permanently removed through baptism. My second grade teacher illustrated this by drawing a circle on the chalkboard to represent the soul, and adding a large mark in the center. This was a soul stained by original sin. Then she erased original sin from the soul, explaining that baptism removes it forever. Personal sin is a different matter.

Personal sin results from the decision of an individual to disobey God and thereby offend him. By committing sin, we deliberately turn away from God's love. Personal sin is repeatable and it can lead to habitual sin by weakening the conscience. It also impacts the family, and society in general, with its far-reaching and damaging effects. Our inclination to sin originated in the Garden of Eden.

The Book of Genesis tells us that when God created the first man and appointed him caretaker of Paradise, he filled the magnificent garden with every kind of creature, species that fly and swim, as well as those that walk and creep. In addition, God planted all manner of trees, fruits, and foliage for sustenance. Finally, seeing man's need for companionship, God provided him with a helpmate, woman. He charged the first family with the care of both the garden and all of the creatures living there.

God blessed the first family, exhorting them to be fruitful and multiply. He was clearly pleased with his work. Everything they needed to sustain a good life had been provided for them. There was only one condition. Adam and Eve were forbidden to eat fruit from the Tree of Knowledge of Good and Evil. To do so, God warned, would result in death. Because they had been given the gift of free will, Adam and Eve were presented with a difficult choice.

Curiosity can be a wonderful thing, but in the case of Adam and Eve it proved their downfall. Led down the path of seduction, Eve was lured by her desire for godly knowledge and power to taste fruit from the forbidden tree. She encouraged Adam to do the same. In disobeying their Creator, they gained personal knowledge of evil and all that it entails. They also felt remorse. Wrapped in their shame, our parents tried to hide themselves among the trees, but no one can hide from the omniscient eye of God.

The immediate consequence of their attempt to achieve equality with God was their fall from his grace. Through their sin of disobedience, sin and its companion, death, became our legacy. Adam and Eve's *original sin* was passed on to all of their progeny, along with its effects.

Because they had set themselves in opposition to God and his grace, Adam and Eve could no longer stay in Paradise. Cast out of the garden that had been their dominion, they forfeited their former privileged life for a demanding life of pain and hardship. Furthermore, Eve would experience painful childbirth and Adam would earn their bread by the sweat of his brow. Worse yet, they lost their intimate relationship with God.

Although baptism cleanses us from original sin once and forever, it does not free us from the effects of our first parents' disobedience. Therefore, we inherit disease, suffering, and death, along with an inclination to commit personal sin. However, as we shall see, God the Father did not abandon us. Because he is all-loving, as well as all-knowing and just, God meted out their punishment tempered with love.

Even as he evicted Adam and Eve from the garden called Paradise, God had a loving plan for mankind's redemption. Setting the serpent in opposition to humans, God foretold that the offspring of a woman would crush him. (Gn 3:15) This is corroborated by the prophet Isaiah, who spoke of the child whose dominion will result in a "peace that has no end." (Is 9:7) Although the scope of God's plan was not clear to our first parents, we now begin to know the fullness of his providence.

The effects of original sin come to us along with further complications caused by the sins of our many ancestors. In their own time, Adam and Eve saw the extensive repercussions of their error, for they had opened the door for evil to enter and roam freely in the pursuit of man's downfall. That first sin ushered in the travails of humankind. Later, Adam and Eve witnessed the terrible effects of personal sin within their own family.The first recorded incident of personal sin in the Bible describes how their son Cain killed his brother Abel in a fit of jealousy and anger. As punishment, God banished Cain from his home and made him a wanderer in a foreign land, separated from both God and family. The misery of the human condition began to unfold.

THE PROVIDENCE OF GOD

Throughout the Old Testament, there are numerous stories of human disobedience and transgressions, with the resulting consequences. Time and again, God's people turned away and suffered the pain of separation from him. Over and over again, Yahweh reached out in justice and in mercy to embrace them, only to watch his children fall again into disobedience.

Even though his people continued to sin and disobey him, the Father fulfilled the promise he had made in the garden. He sent the love-gift of his own Son to change the hearts of errant humans and to guarantee their salvation through his death for their sins.

Jesus is the Healer sent into the world to show us the compassionate love of the Father. During his public ministry, he not only spoke of that love, he demonstrated it by forgiving sinners, by healing illness, blindness, and deafness, by casting out demons, and even by reversing death. His love for us culminated with the suffering and agony that led to his own death upon a cross.

The pain that Jesus endured during the crucifixion was more than physical. He drank from a cup of agony. The cup was filled with the sinfulness of *all* people, from the very beginning until the end of time. Sinless himself, he not only bore the terrible weight of our sins, he died to atone for them. Then he conquered death by his resurrection, proving he was truly God. Finally, he returned to his Father in heaven to await our arrival.

Through baptism, we became children of God and co-heirs of the Kingdom with Jesus. Jesus guaranteed our place in heaven, and with perfect love he offers many avenues of healing for our broken lives.

HOPE FOR THE HUMAN CONDITION

Even though the Father has claimed us as own his children, we still suffer from the *effects* of personal sins. These include the effects of our sins, as well as those of others. They also include the sins of our ancestors, the effects of which are passed down through the generations. The damaging consequences of personal sin can be experienced spiritually, emotionally, mentally, and physically. Some effects of generational sin are easily recognized. A significant indicator is a repetitious pattern of affliction from generation to generation.

People often turn to generational healing when other prayers for healing have been unsuccessful. These are the persistent petitioners who stand on Jesus promise:

> I tell you most solemnly,
> anything you ask for from the Father
> he will grant in my name...
> Ask and you will receive,
> and so your joy will be complete.

(Jn 16:23-24)

GATHERING THE FAMILY STORY

Several years ago, my husband and I visited Ireland, the place of my father's birth. Equipped with only his birth certificate and the name of a village so small it did not appear on the map, we actually found the farm where he was born. As I stood on that windswept hilltop, on barren land rich in stones, I experienced a sense of completeness. An ancient voice within me spoke to my spirit, "This is where you belong. Now, you have come home."

While we stood there absorbing the vista of rolling green hills and cloud-dotted blue skies, a neighbor related stories about my ancestors that he had heard from his father. I began to appreciate the worth of family history. In Ireland, the old-timers remember, and they keep memory alive by sharing their stories from generation to generation.

In a nearby village, we searched for the birthplace of my father's mother, Mary Anne. She died when I was only three months old and many of her children died in childhood or in early adulthood. Since I knew my Irish ancestors primarily from stories I had heard, I was hoping to learn more about their lives in Ireland.

I felt uncomfortable about knocking on the doors of strangers, so I waited in the car while my husband went to the door of the little farmhouse. The woman who appeared at the door looked my way and motioned to me. As I walked towards the cottage, she smiled and welcomed me, "Come in! Come in! I knew you were family as soon as I saw you. You look just like Joe's sister, Delia." I was stunned. Until that moment, she hadn't known that I existed. Yet she recognized me instantly.

In the parlor, we met her husband, my father's first cousin. As we sat and visited, I was struck by Joe's resemblance to my dad. They both had the same gentle demeanor and similar facial features. I learned that reading and the love of books is a family trait we all shared. I have since heard of yet another cousin in this family who, though well into her nineties, is still an avid reader.

Through the stories I heard that day, it became clear to me that these shared traits and features could not be mere coincidence. My attributes did not come solely from influences within my immediate family. They were passed down through the generations. The grandmother I hadn't known emerged as a strong-willed but courageous person, a gifted storyteller, and a survivor. I am pleased that there is something of Mary Anne in me.

THE GOAL OF FAMILY TREE HEALING

Your life is closely tied to your family and, like it or not, you also acquired both positive and negative family characteristics. Your family heritage includes attitudes and emotional patterns, beliefs and prejudices, talents and abilities, and more. Whether or not you were raised by your natural parents, you inherited from them specific genetic markers which influence your life and health.

As science advances in the study of genetics, there is interest and hope in preventing many serious illnesses through the early recognition of such markers. A great deal more research is needed to identify possible genetic factors in life-threatening diseases before they can be eradicated. Meanwhile, on the spiritual level it is recognized that the prescriptions for healing destructive spiritual and emotional problems, which often contribute to physical illnesses, are found in the Bible.

The goal of family healing is to discover the roots of iniquity and brokenness in ancestors and to discern their connection, if any, with the afflictions of present generations. You begin with what you already know about your family. Then, with enlightenment from the Holy Spirit, you explore the family history for patterns of illness, negative attitudes, destructive behavior, and other problems.

Through the inspiration of the Holy Spirit, you will discern how to pray for your family's generational healing. Then, in a spirit of repentance and apology, you will pray for family healing through the power of Jesus, who died for our sins.

You need not be Catholic to have a Mass (Liturgy) said for your family tree. For those who are uncomfortable with this approach, we will explore other ways to pray for your family's healing. God's ability to heal is unlimited.

At the beginning of your family research, the unanswered questions can feel overwhelming. The exploration of just one life, with its twistings, turnings, and blocked passages, can seem like a labyrinth, a complex network of interconnected paths. The way in is deceptively easy, but finding the right path through it is difficult. The journey is seductive. You can become so enthralled with the investigation that you lose sight of your purpose. Since your intention is healing for your family line, finding your way is essential.

Deep family healing invites you to explore, not only your own life, but also those of other relatives and deceased ancestors. In order to reexamine the past and bring closure and healing to old issues, you must be willing to enter into the labyrinth. The mythical Theseus marked his passage by unraveling a ball of thread as he journeyed deep into the labyrinth to slay the beast known as the Minotaur. The thread helped him complete his task and exit safely.

Your journey through generational healing requires persistence, prayer, and a bright unwavering light for the dark passages. The beasts you slay may be your own inner demons, as well as those of afflicted relatives who lived before you. During this process, you will gain a new appreciation and love for your ancestors, and you will experience deep gratitude for the gifts and talents you have inherited from them.

Like the ball of thread that Theseus carried, this book helps you to stay focused and organized as you research your family history. The Holy Spirit provides the necessary discernment and understanding to guide your prayers. The Light of Christ illuminates your journey and ultimately heals any remnants of family brokenness you uncover. He is the fulfillment of the Father's promise to abundantly bless your family tree.

WHAT REALLY HAPPENED IN THE GARDEN?

Read Genesis Chapter 3. As the editor of a tabloid newspaper, you must select the headline which best describes the events in the Garden of Eden. Which headline is the most accurate?

SIN IN THE GARDEN

ROUND 1, GAME OF LIFE: SERPENT 2, HUMANS 0

OUTCASTS EVICTED FROM PARADISE

SERPENT IN TREE CONQUERS HUMANITY

FDA RECALLS EDEN APPLES:
  HARMFUL TO SPIRITUAL HEALTH

FASHION AND FIG LEAVES:
  DESIGNS FOR THE NEW EVE

HUMAN ERROR: GOD PROMISES REDEMPTION

Only one conveys the truth: God's promise of redemption.

TO WHOM SHALL WE GO?

To whom shall we go, Lord? You are the source of eternal life. Jesus, Creator of life, thank you for the gift of my life, and for the blessing of my family. Help me, Lord, to fully appreciate your wisdom in choosing my parents and my ancestors. I lift up my entire family for your blessing and healing, so that we may grow in unity and in love. Lord, you have the power to heal across the boundaries of time because you live in eternity. I pray that you will reward my ancestors for their virtues and good intentions, and forgive their failings, bringing them into the fullness of your grace and peace. Amen.

Chapter 1.

1. Myra Vanderpool Gormley, *Family Diseases: Are You at Risk?* (MD: Genealogical Publishing Co., 1989).

2. THE MAJESTY OF GOD

"Where your treasure is,
there will your heart be also." (Mt 6:21)

Faith is an essential element in prayers for healing. Faith is your belief in God, the mark of your personal relationship with him. It enables you to have complete trust that he keeps his promises. Faith is the glue that keeps you from falling apart, even in times of darkness.

Have you ever tried to describe God? My dictionary defines God as "the supreme or ultimate reality" and "the Being perfect in power, wisdom, and goodness whom men worship as creator and ruler of the universe."[1] True enough, but that definition does not begin to depict God as I know him today. With all of the words at my disposal, I can find only one that comes close to describing him. That word is love.

At one time, I thought of God the Father as a punishing God, a mean-spirited Santa Claus figure who wrote down and kept track of every wrong thing I did. Then, at a pivotal point in my life, I finally came to know the merciful love of God the Father. He truly is a loving father who treasures me as his child. He loves me no matter what I do. Even when I sin and fall from grace, he goes right on loving me. His love is so constant and faithful, it humbles me.

Because he reveals himself to me as the very essence of goodness and love, I want more and more to be like him. I recognize that in my poor human state, I can never be worthy of God's love, but I keep trying to live my life in a way that glorifies my Father. He has unbelievable patience.

The generosity of my Father in heaven provides for all of my needs in this life. He knows my imperfections and my weaknesses and he also knows that I need divine help to overcome them. Not only did he send his own Son, Jesus, to redeem the sins of all people, he gave us Jesus to walk with us and to be both friend and healer. The Holy Spirit, flowing out of the love of the Father and Jesus, assists us as guide and inspiration, helper and comforter.

THE HEART OF GOD

The heart of God longs for an exclusive relationship with each one of us. His plan is for us to know him in a deeply personal way, to live lives of loyalty and service that give glory to him, and to spend eternity with him in heaven.

I believe that God gives us unlimited opportunities to fulfill that plan, forgiving us time and again and loving us unconditionally. The Father has given us everything we need to survive the difficulties of this life. We are the children of royalty through no merit of our own, and our ultimate inheritance surpasses anything the world can offer. With the help of his grace, we can strive to become the perfected gems in the crown of God that we are meant to be.

When we know God from this perspective, we can trust in his mercy. We are his very own children, made in his image. He has known us from the very beginning. He called us by name. He does not punish us with sickness. Rather, he wants to heal our sickness and brokenness because he is a God of love that knows no limits.

Sometimes we misunderstand Yahweh (the Old Testament name for God) and form wrong impressions about him. His justice and power are tempered by love and mercy, as shown in the sacrifice of his own Son to redeem our souls. His freely-given love and mercy are essential components of God's character and should not be overlooked.

YAHWEH IS A PERSONAL GOD

The Book of Exodus describes how Yahweh established a covenant with the Jewish people. In *Reading the Old Testament: An Introduction*, Lawrence Boadt, C.S.P. describes this covenant relationship as an unbreakable union between the people and Yahweh. God pledges his love and mercy to the people and in return, he expects their worship, faithfulness, and obedience. God does not guarantee that we will always be victorious in battle, or that we will have great wealth. "...more often it [*the covenant*] describes the blessing that trust in the Lord will bring:.. [*including*[permanent peace and the joy of knowing God is near."[2]

The roots of Christianity exist in the Jewish religion and its traditions. When we consider the hereditary effects of the sins of our ancestors, we also need to remember that God promised blessings on those who love, trust, and obey him. His benevolence makes generational healing possible.

The concept of generational healing is a response to the words of Yahweh to Moses on Mount Sinai. Presenting him with the Ten Commandments for the Israelites, he said:

> I am Yahweh your God who brought you out of the land of Egypt, out of the house of slavery. You shall have no gods except me. You shall not make yourself a carved image or any likeness of anything in heaven or on earth beneath or in the waters under the earth; you shall not bow down to them or serve them. For I, Yahweh your God, am a jealous God and I punish[3] the father's fault in the sons, the grandsons, and the great-grandsons of those who hate me; but I show kindness to thousands of those who love me and keep my commandments. (Ex 20:5-6)

Faith-filled believers who live godly lives are seen by God as those who love him. To these and their progeny he extends untold blessings. In the context of the first commandment, which demands our allegiance to the one true God, Yahweh characterizes sinners as those who fail to love him by turning away and worshiping false gods. To these sinners he extends punishment to the third or fourth generation.

Perhaps you are thinking, "That was the Old Testament! What does that have to do with me and my family? We belong to the New Covenant!" Jesus secured our inheritance as heirs of heaven. He did not take away our free will, nor did he negate the precepts of the Old Testament.

JESUS FULFILLS THE LAW

In his Sermon on the Mount, Jesus proclaimed that he came, not to abolish the law but rather to fulfill it. (Mt 5:17-19) Jesus clarified this for the Pharisees, who prided themselves on their strict and legalistic interpretation of laws and oral tradition, when he said:

You must love the Lord your God with all your heart, with all your soul, and with all your mind. This is the greatest and the first commandment. The second resembles it: You must love your neighbour as yourself. On these two commandments hang the whole Law, and the Prophets also. (Mt 22:37-40)

On the surface, it appears that Jesus simplified matters. All we have to do is love God, ourselves, and one another. In reality, the love required by Christ's commandments sets a higher standard of compliance than the Old Covenant. In Matthew 5, Jesus explains that the law of love demands far more than obedience. His counsel includes the requirement to turn the other cheek when we are struck, to give to anyone who asks, and above all, to forgive one another.

You have learnt how it was said: You must love your neighbour and hate your enemy. But I say this to you: love your enemies and pray for those who persecute you; in this way you will be sons of your Father in heaven.... You must therefore be perfect just as your heavenly Father is perfect. (Mt 5:43-45, 48)

LOVE DEFINES THE LAW

Love defines the law. God *is* love. He loves us unconditionally, in spite of our moral weakness and our failings. When we commit serious sin, however, we turn away from God to embrace evil. Jesus warns us that we cannot serve two masters. (Mt 6:24) When we choose a life of sin, we put our eternal life with God at grave risk.

Our just and loving God will not tolerate our fellowship with the evil one, who is the antithesis of love. Yahweh warned that generations would suffer for the sin of idolatry, and idolatry is not limited to the ancient pagan worship of statues made from molten metal. We cross a dangerous line when we allow our fascinations to become obsessions. Anything that we value above God can become idolatry. Idolatry can include giving honor to false gods, demons, money, pleasure, power, ancestors, material goods, celebrities, the Internet, and the stock market, to name just a few examples.

In addition to idolatry, the first commandment forbids superstition, sorcery, and occult activities. The practice of divination, the seeking of knowledge through occult powers, is one of the subtle ways that evil usurps our loyalty to God and acquires a grasp on the soul. Even when the occult is approached in the innocence of childhood or as a form of entertainment, it can yield calamitous spiritual consequences that may not be evident immediately.

SIN HAS CONSEQUENCES

Sin always has consequences. Whether you consider it punishment, or a visitation of the natural result of wrongdoing, the reality is that when a person sins, others suffer from the effects of that sin. The effects impact the family, as well as future generations, by setting off a chain reaction.

Society requires punishment in jail when a man robs a bank. This is true even though he later repents and receives God's forgiveness. Meanwhile, his family suffers because of his sinful action. In addition to feeling shame and anger, they may suffer hardship and poverty. The criminal's children, who have been deprived of their father's presence, may believe society "owes" them. Perhaps they will pursue lives of crime themselves, seeking the "easy" way to obtain what they have been denied. The father's sin has affected his children, and possibly his grandchildren.

Violence begets violence, whether it has its roots in an abusive home situation or in the "gang" mentality that plagues impoverished neighborhoods. According to therapist and author Susan

Forward, Ph.D., "Physical abusers themselves often come from families in which abuse was the norm." As an abused child, a person may learn to use violence to manage strong negative feelings and overwhelming emotions, such as anger. When that inner rage is triggered in the adult, abuse is sometimes directed towards a child who serves as a stand-in for the abuser's parent.[4]

The generational consequences of abuse are corroborated by John Bradshaw, who explains that child abuse can result if the parents' needs were not met in childhood. Bradshaw describes the many complex ways that unhealthy behavior patterns, such as alcoholism and abuse, are assimilated and carried from one generation to the next. With a five-generation genogram, he shows the repetition of these and other behavior patterns.[5]

As part of the healing process, destructive cycles must be broken. While recovery may be aided by therapy and 12-step programs, it is God who changes hearts. Charles L. Whitfield, M.D., an expert in the field of recovery issues, states: "I believe that spirituality is crucial in achieving full recovery from any medical or psychological condition, and especially for discovering and ultimately liberating the Child Within, our Real True Self."[6]

In cases of physical illness, there can be multiple causes. Some illnesses have psychological causes. An unhealthy lifestyle can precipitate illness, and a weakened immune system can make one vulnerable to disease. Genetic components may predispose a person to certain illnesses. In addition, there can be environmental causes. In the case of mental disturbances, emotional problems, attitudes and prejudices, and even addictions, links to ancestors often can be identified.

We turn to Jesus, the Healer, to restore the health of our families. Our prayers are directed at the inherited *effects* of sins committed by ancestors, as we seek forgiveness and reconciliation with our ancestors and with God. In later chapters, we will consider other ways that the effects of sin and brokenness infect generations of a family.

A PERSONAL ASSESSMENT

Label this section of your notebook: *SELF-INVENTORY*.

1. What do you treasure the most? Make a list.
2. How would you describe God to a group of young children? Write a description of God as you know him.
3. Is your relationship with God satisfying to you?
4. What, if anything, would you like to change about it?
5. Describe your relationship with Jesus.
6. Are you comfortable in that relationship?
7. Describe your prayer life.
8. Do you read the Bible? How often?
9. On a page labeled family, make a list of the primary members of your family. Include spouse, children, parents, brothers and sisters, grandparents, and great-grandparents.
10. Make notations by the names of relatives you believe need spiritual, emotional, or physical healing.

LORD, HEAR MY PRAYER

Dear God, I come before you today, just as I am. I can hide nothing from you. You know me through and through, my strengths as well as my weaknesses. You also know my family and our need for deep healing. Help us to draw closer to you, Lord. I believe that you keep your promises and I place my trust in your love and mercy. Amen.

Chapter 2.

1. *Webster's Seventh New Collegiate Dictionary* (MA: G. & C. Merriam Co., 1972), 358.

2. Lawrence Boadt, *Reading the Old Testament: An Introduction* (NY/Mahwah, NJ: Paulist Press, 1984), 175.

3. In the Latin Vulgate, the Hebrew word *paqad* was translated "visit" (not "punish") by St. Jerome. An accomplished linguist and scholar, Jerome is credited with remaining true to the meaning of the original Hebrew text in his translation of the Old Testament.

4. Susan Forward, Ph.D., *Toxic Parents* (NY: Bantam Books, 1989), 120.

5. John Bradshaw, *Bradshaw On: The Family* (FL: Health Communications, Inc., 1988), 62-63, 67.

6. Charles L. Whitfield, M.D., *Healing the Child Within: Discovery and Recovery for Adult Children of Dysfunctional Families* (FL: Health Communications Inc., 1987), 8.

3. YOUR FAMILY TREE

"Honor the tree that gives you shelter."
(Danish proverb)

Tending a garden connects your soul to God. As you participate in the creation of beauty and watch seeds you have sown reach their full potential, you become his collaborator.

Just as gardening can bring you closer to God, healing your family is akin to having God's finger on the pulse of your soul. He already knows about the problems that concern you and he offers you his healing touch. What he waits for is your awareness of the need for healing and your active cooperation in his process.

For me, the best part of gardening comes after the hard work of digging and planting. I watch with anticipation for results, compensating for my lack of a green thumb with an immense amount of hope and expectation. Perhaps it is this same trait that attracted me to genealogy.

Initially, I was prompted to explore our family's history to find help for my daughter's schizophrenia. Her illness manifested suddenly in 1979, after I was diagnosed with a rare and terminal cancer. Her inability to deal with the crisis of my impending death brought on her complete mental breakdown. A month later, my cancer was miraculously healed through prayer, but my daughter remained lost in a world of mental confusion.

I first learned about generational healing in 1980, during a trip to the Orient. My husband and I had the privilege of hearing Jesuit priests Matthew and Dennis Linn speak at Tokyo University. They told about the importance of praying for the deceased and described the healing that parents experienced through special prayers for their miscarried or aborted babies. What interested me most then was their description of other healings that had occurred after families offered the Eucharist for their dead ancestors.

The most startling story we heard that day concerned a schizophrenic who experienced auditory sounds and voices reminiscent of a battle at sea. The patient's odd and unexplainable symptoms included profuse sweating and a perception of burning sulfur. Psychiatrist Kenneth McAll discovered that the patient's ancestors included numerous pirates. Among them was a pirating sea captain by the same name who had died in the late 1500s. Though hospitalized some distance away from the Eucharist that was offered for his ancestors, the man experienced a spontaneous cure of his schizophrenia.

Years passed before I finally located additional information on generational healing. The books in print today were not yet available. When I finally compiled our family tree for generational healing, I was greatly helped in my discernment by the guidance of the Holy Spirit. My family history notes continue to grow as the Holy Spirit helps me to recognize the roots of patterns within our family that need additional prayer. Family healing is an ongoing process.

ROOTS AND SELF-UNDERSTANDING

Once we begin to own the tendencies we acquired from our ancestors, we embark on a journey of greater self-understanding and healing. In spite of dramatic changes in family lifestyles over recent decades, we are still deeply connected to our relatives and ancestors. Although we live in an age that celebrates individuality, family roots are more significant than many people realize.

The roots of a tree grow out of sight underground, but they provide a system of nurturing and anchoring which determines the basic health of the tree. Other environmental factors contribute to that health, but sound roots are essential to a strong tree.

A forest is a neighborhood of many trees that coexist in a complex structure of interdependence. A tree that stands tall and straight—a tree that flourishes and withstands all manner of weather—has roots that live deep in healthy soil. By the same token, a tree that is easily uprooted by wind and precipitation may have a shallow or damaged root system. Yet, even fallen trees contribute organic matter to the forest floor, supporting the growth of new trees to replace the old.

What has all this to do with family healing? More than you might suspect. Families, like individuals, come in many shapes and sizes. Some have been undernourished. Their roots may have suffered damage. Defective genetic strains contribute to physical and emotional illness. Families can become bruised and disfigured just like trees, and sometimes the severity of the damage goes unrecognized for generations. There is, however, one big difference. The health of a family can be restored. It is never too late or too difficult to repair the family tree.

HOW DOES YOUR GARDEN GROW?

A garden, generally speaking, is a cultivated plot of ground planted with flowers, vegetables, shrubs, and trees. It may or may not be surrounded by a fence. The planting of a formal garden requires extensive planning and preparation.

While you can make the decision whether or not to have children, you cannot choose your parents and ancestors. Even if you could divorce yourself from your forebears, you have already been influenced by the past, with all that it contains. What you can do, however, is present the past to Jesus for his healing and blessing.

Each one of us is as special and distinctly beautiful in God's sight as the most exquisite flower, and the same is true of all your family members. God loves all of us impartially, seeing our potential to become more like him.

We often fail to recognize and appreciate the beauty of others because we have not yet learned to see them through God's eyes. At times, your family may seem more like an uncultivated garden, growing wild and untended. Think of a field full of rocks, overgrown with tangled vines, and dotted with colorful wildflowers intermixed with weeds.

As you survey your family, you will find similar diversity. While some relatives are strong and well-grounded like stones, they may be weighty and difficult to move. Others may seem like wildflowers, each one beautiful in its own way but lacking permanence. Some may remind you of blades of grass, bending whichever way the wind blows. Perhaps the lives and problems of some relatives seem hopelessly entangled because of their co-dependent behaviors. Others may seem like weeds you would prefer to discard. Yet even these have value in God's plan.

How can we account for such variety within a single family? Each one of us enters the world as an infant, trusting and innocent, totally dependent upon others. In the early years of childhood, we give our love freely and completely. It is all we have to give. Initially, we can only communicate by crying or not crying, and we quickly train our caregivers to feed us and keep us comfortable. Our physical needs are basic and simple: food and shelter. Our most important human need is love.

A child, eager for life's journey, plunges in with undaunted enthusiasm and curiosity. Along the way, however, trust can become corrupted, innocence may be defiled, eagerness can diminish, curiosity may languish, and the inner person becomes battered and bruised. Depending on the extent of the wounding, the second half of a person's life may be spent in the quest for healing of damages incurred in the first half.

Prayers for inner healing are effective for many of the hurts that stem from childhood. Some emotional wounds are unexplainable. They seem to bear no relation to the events of a person's life. The same can be true of physical illness. Doctors are sometimes baffled when a patient reports symptoms that cannot be linked to a physical cause. Emotional or physical problems that defy medical treatment and healing prayer may have deeper roots.

While the study of genetics offers hope for the future prevention or cure of strongly resistant physical diseases, there is also a growing awareness of the generational factor in some physical, emotional, and mental problems. Doctor Kenneth McAll, a pioneer in generational healing through prayer, reports surprising healings that have resulted from generational prayer.[1]

Following McAll's approach, some clergymen, therapists, prayer ministers, and family historians have documented recognizable patterns that are passed down from generation to generation. These include family dysfunction, behavior disorders of all sorts, mental depression, some physical illnesses, and more.

When family problems still remain after prayer, counseling, medical treatment, and other reasonable efforts have been tried, there may be unexplained links to ancestors through the bloodline.

Specific prayers for ancestral healing often result in visible cures among living members of the family. Our prayers for deceased family and friends are completely in accord with Church teaching, which tells us that we are one body in Christ.

THE MYSTICAL BODY OF CHRIST

Christianity teaches that death will no longer exist when Jesus comes in his final glory. It was a tradition to pray for the dead in the earliest days of Christianity. In fact, this custom predates Christ.

In the Old Testament, when Judas Maccabees and his soldiers prepared to have fallen Jewish soldiers returned to their ancestors' tombs, they discovered pagan amulets on the bodies of the dead. Believing in life with God after death, they prayed, asking God to blot out these idolatrous sins of the dead. Then Judas took up a collection so that an atonement sacrifice could be offered for them in Jerusalem. (2 Macc 12:38-46)

We do not live in a vacuum. Our lives are interconnected with the lives of others, both living and dead. In explaining our relationship with the Body of Christ, the *Catechism of the Catholic Church* describes the "communion of saints" thus: "...some of his disciples are pilgrims on earth. Others have died and are being purified, while still others are in glory, contemplating in full light, God himself triune and one, exactly as he is."[2]

The Catechism explains that those closely united to Christ in heaven continue to intercede for us with God the Father. It seems logical that those who loved us in life will continue to love us and pray for us in heaven. Our well-being is still important to them, and in heaven, face to face with Divinity, they have access to the ear of God.

The souls of the dead undergoing purification, those who do not yet enjoy the full presence of God's glory, need our ongoing prayers. Caught somewhere between heaven and earth, they rely on us to pray for them.

During the Catholic Liturgy, we pray for the dead as well as for the living. In recommending that we pray to free the dead from their sins, the Catechism explains that our prayers help departed souls who are incapable of helping themselves. Our prayers obtain for them the fullness of God's healing and they, in turn, intercede on our behalf. We are powerfully connected with those family members who have died, just as we are with our living relatives. Even if we did not know them, our lives have been deeply affected by theirs. We are related to them through our bloodline. While our bodies contain DNA unique to us, they also contain genetic markers passed down through generations of our families.

Your prayers for family healing are an appropriate response to God's declaration that he punishes the sins of the fathers, while extending his blessings to those who love him and keep his commandments. Your prayers acknowledge and rely upon his mercy and forgiveness.

BEGIN AT THE BEGINNING

To prepare for healing your family tree, you will research the past. Important clues that help facilitate family healing can usually be discovered in your family's history. Your task is to identify repeated instances of specific health problems and any serious transgressions by ancestors, the effects of which might be an underlying cause of physical, mental, emotional, or spiritual disease in living members of your family. This is not as difficult as it might seem. There are many avenues of investigation that will help your research. The first step is to assemble information that is already known about your family. The exercise at the end of this chapter will guide you through this task.

An inexpensive notebook with dividers will help you keep your data organized. This notebook is an important tool. As you acquire information from multiple sources, you will be keeping notes on the lives of different family members. Since genealogical information has a way of multiplying, an organized approach is essential. (*see* Appendix II)

Try to avoid distraction by irrelevant details that can lead you astray from your primary goal of family healing. While such facts are interesting, it helps to ask yourself if they are pertinent to the healing. If not, simply note extraneous information on a separate page for future reference.

As you gather family history, be alert for patterns. In addition to repetitious disease or transgressions, look for patterns such as: negative attitudes or character traits, behavior, prejudices, beliefs, remarkable coincidences, criminal behavior, addiction, mental imbalance or psychosis, occult practices, and sinfulness.

Do not overlook positive attributes such as loyalty and spiritual strength in family members. These important aspects of your heredity help to offset negative influences. Other facts to note are relatives who died traumatic deaths (murders, accidents, suicides), infants who died early, and pregnancies that did not reach full term (miscarriages, stillbirths, and abortions). You should include anyone who was not reconciled with God at the time of death, and those who did not receive a Christian burial.

You may discover that other family members do not share your interest in collecting the family history. They may fail to recognize the importance you place on this research. Nevertheless, your tactful questions will probably result in the kind of information you are seeking. It is amazing how quickly memories are generated and shared during casual discussions that begin, "Remember when...."

Do not be surprised if family members have different recollections of the same events. Memory is selective and perception is unique in each individual. We tend to remember the things that are important to us, and sometimes we bury memories that are unpleasant or bothersome. Memories can also become distorted.

Every family has skeletons in the closet, secrets that are kept hidden from other family members. They are the result of misplaced efforts to protect and preserve reputations, to shield overly sensitive members from hurtful information, and in some cases this is a type of denial. "If we don't talk about it, it didn't happen."

Skeletons in the family closet usually represent problems that require deep healing. The initial reason for secrecy may have been forgotten after the key to the closet was thrown away. While bringing the truth to light requires skill and delicacy, it also results in healing. We cannot rewrite history but we can try to see the errors and blunders of the past with empathy.

The Bridges of Madison County[3] gives a classic example of family secrets coming to light. The film opens with the adult children sorting through their mother's personal belongings after her death. Their discovery of a journal reveals a secret about their mother they had never known. Their varied reactions of disbelief, shock, anger, hurt, betrayal, and finally empathy with her situation, are characteristic of human nature.

By opening the closet and revealing her secret, the mother invites her children's understanding and forgiveness. She also offers them an opportunity to grow. One wonders what might have happened had she spoken to them about her indiscretions while she was still alive. She might have helped them to make more honest decisions in their own lives. Or perhaps she would have alienated them completely. In either case, a different story would have resulted and healing still may have been needed.

Denial, continuing anger, and unresolved grief are factors that need to be considered as you research your family history. How has your family handled major crises? The answer to that question may lead you to uncover areas of deep woundedness.

Denial is one way that people handle crisis. Often, a person with terminal illness is encircled by hushed secrecy within the family. The sick person avoids any discussion of the prognosis for fear of upsetting others, while family members find it equally difficult to broach the subject. Everyone may pretend nothing serious is wrong. Locked in silence, they are all deprived of the mutual comfort and support they desperately need. Fear and uncertainty rob them of the precious opportunity to say the loving words they need to share.

Disasters, sickness, and death often lead one to question God. People may wonder if they are being punished for some misdeed or omission. Anger is one way of handling the crisis. That anger may be directed at God, toward the sick or dying person for not getting well, or at oneself. Given our human nature, we don't worry much about eternity when things are going well. However, serious misfortune or grave illness plunge us into the reality.

Life on earth is uncertain and temporary, and death confronts us with our own mortality. For this reason, some people are not comfortable discussing the subject of death. The death of a loved one is a terrible loss. If the grief process has not had closure, just remembering the death of a relative can bring back all the pain associated with the loss. This certainly indicates a need for healing prayer.

You may be seeking family healing because of a current crisis in your family. Or perhaps you are at the midpoint of life and beginning to question the past as you search for life's meaning. The midlife quest can be characterized by intensity and a sense of newness. It can also take the form of a midlife crisis or breakdown. In either case, spiritual growth and healing are possible.

The search for family history is seductive. The more you know, the more you want to know. It is easy to become lost in the family forest. Stay focused on your original purpose, which is the healing of family defects. What sets your quest apart from ordinary genealogical research is your desire for family healing.

Make daily prayer an integral part of your research process. You are asking God to breathe life back into the dry bones of your ancestors. Call upon the guidance of the Holy Spirit to lead you through the research process and to keep you focused on the healing love of Jesus.

NAMING THE PROBLEM

Label this section of your notebook *The Problem*.

1. Complete the sentence: My family is...

2. In order to solve a problem, you need to identify and understand it. Here are some questions to consider:

a. What serious health problems drain your family's energy and resources? These might include: cardiovascular disease, Alzheimer's disease, cancer, HIV or AIDS, mental illness, neurological disorders, birth defects, respiratory illness, or other disabling illnesses.

b. Does your family suffer because of addictive behavior in one or more members? Addictive behavior (*any habit which is out of control*) includes: alcoholism, substance abuse, gambling, eating disorders, sexual addiction, and workaholism. Addiction affects everyone within the family circle, not just the addict.

c. Does moral weakness interfere with family harmony? Deception, immorality, criminal behavior, and grave sinfulness are examples of moral weakness.

d. List any negative family traits, such as gossiping, backbiting, lying, and laziness.

e. List positive family traits, such as generosity, sincerity, courage, moral strength, spirituality, honesty, and strong principles.

f. Describe your family's spiritual life.

3. Try to clarify in your mind the most urgent problem that affects your family today. Is there more than one issue? Prioritize them. Write a brief description of the illness or family situation of greatest concern: physical disease, mental illness, addictive behavior, family feuding, divorce, phobias, neurotic behavior, or other concerns.

Read Ez 36:16-37.

A NEW HEART AND A NEW SPIRIT

I ask you, Jesus, for the guidance of your Spirit as I research my family history. Enlighten me. Help me to recognize the virtues of my ancestors, as well as any negative patterns of sin or brokenness that have passed down through the generations of my family.

As I research my family tree, grant me compassionate understanding and a forgiving heart. Help me to love the unlovable, to bear the unbearable, and to pray constantly for all of my relatives, both living and dead. Amen.

Chapter 3.

1   Kenneth McAll, M.D., psychiatrist and author of books on generational healing. (*see* Books).

2.   "Lumen Gentium 49," cf. Eph 4:16; *Catechism of the Catholic Church* (NY: Doubleday, 1995), 270-272.

3.   Based on the novel by Robert James Waller.

Rooted in Jesus

4. THE COMPLEXITIES OF FAMILY LIFE

"...everything that we are and have, even the
painful and mysterious, is God's generous gift."[1]

As small children, we think that all families are like our own. Gradually, our boundaries expand and we begin to see differences. Some families have single parents. Others don't. Not all parents are married to one another. One survey reported that by 1994, cohabitation without marriage was the norm in 50% of American households, compared with 10% in 1965.[2] Clearly, the trend away from the traditional "nuclear" family is increasing. Meanwhile, many children are being raised by grandparents, and some by couples in same-sex relationships.

In many families, both parents work, while in others one or both parents stay home all the time. In some homes there is laughter and fun. In others, you feel tension the moment you walk through the front door.

Is your family characterized by healthy, well-balanced, highly educated, professionally successful, happy people who all work together in harmony for the good of the family structure? Probably not. There are no perfect families, just as there are no perfect people. Only God is perfect. Human nature is weak and imperfect. People with the best intentions have faults, and illness shows no respect for bank account, moral integrity, or holiness. Like imperfection, it affects people of every age, color, condition, and walk of life.

Within a family, even though every member is a distinct individual, there are recognizable features and traits. What family characteristics do you possess? You might have Uncle Henry's nose or Grandma Betty's smile. You might share your father's temper or your mother's anxiety. Perhaps you have a gift for art or music, or a talent for analytical thinking. One family member may be a gifted auto mechanic, another may excel in mathematics, while yet another shines in the field of human relations.

Individual families are shaped by their history and their culture, but the basic family structure is a sociological grouping of people who share common ancestry. In the narrowest traditional sense, a family consists of one or more adults who cooperate in raising children. The adults might be married parents, stepparents, single parents, older siblings, grandparents, other relatives, close friends, or foster parents.

Ideally, the family is our nurturing and loving support system, as well as the primary social group in which we learn and grow. The reality is that we learn many things growing up within a family, but the learning environment may fall short of ideal. Some lessons are learned in spite of our family situation. For everyone who wants to raise a family just the way Mom and Dad did, there are probably many more with the opposite viewpoint. Theories of parenting change with the seasons, or at least with the decades, and in spite of the many styles of childrearing proposed, no one has yet come up with the perfect answer. As you research your own family's history, you will begin to appreciate its uniqueness.

CHARTING YOUR FAMILY HISTORY

In your quest to heal your family tree, you will explore and chart the history of your family. This is done not with the intention of laying blame on one person or another, but rather with the goal of identifying those ancestors most in need of prayer and healing.

We live in an age when counseling and therapy are readily available. Subjects that once were taboo are now discussed openly, but this was not always the case. In the past, many issues that required healing were carried to the grave, unresolved. Even today, some people with deep inner pain prefer to keep it hidden.

As you investigate your family's history, it is important to be sensitive to the feelings of others. Your goal is to bring healing, not to create additional hurt. You may wonder how the construction of a family tree can provide useful information about your family. This will become more apparent as you learn to record and work with your data in a structured format called a *genogram*. The genogram is like a map in an underground rail station. It shows where you are today, but it also details routes the family has already taken, in a way that makes connections more readily apparent. What you learn from the genogram can help you make better decisions in the future.

In addition to charting your family history on the genogram, you will assign separate pages in your notebook for each branch on the family tree. There you will record the dates of births, marriages, and deaths for each family member. You will also note other details, including divorces, immigration facts, accidents, serious illnesses, and causes of death.

Taken individually, each detail or event may not seem significant. However, when all of these elements are carefully studied on the genogram, a larger more powerful story emerges.

THE FACT-FINDING ADVENTURE

Before my first visit to Ireland, I had no experience in genealogical research. My only genealogical document was a certified copy of my father's birth certificate.[3] It provided his name, date of birth, his parent's names, mother's maiden name, father's occupation, the village in which they lived, and the location of the registering town, district, and county. It also gave the date his birth was registered.

At the library in the town of Castlebar, Ireland, I gained additional information from a microfilm of the 1901 Census. The story of my research shows the extent of detail that can be obtained from such records. When the details are organized and given thoughtful reflection, a family story emerges.

Form A of the 1901 Census for County Mayo in Ireland revealed that the small farming village of Devleash was comprised of nine tracts of land. The head of each family (landholder) was listed, along with particulars of the property.

My ancestors' house was described as a private dwelling, made of stone, brick or concrete, with three outbuildings for the farm. On our visit to Devleash the previous day, we had explored the ruins of the original house. The walls had been constructed from stones gathered from the fields. Since the tenants used whatever was at hand, they probably secured bundles of thatch for the roof. Wood or other perishable material were other possible choices, as opposed to the slate, iron or tile found on more expensive houses. The census described a cottage with two rooms and two windows on the front. Like the neighboring houses, this was categorized as a "Class 3" house.

Seven family members were listed as occupants of this two-room stone cottage. Form B, a separate page in the census, listed the names, sex, and age (on last birthday) of individual family members, the county or country where they were born, their relationship to the head of the family, whether or not they were married, their religion, whether or not they could read and write, and whether they spoke English, Irish, or both. It also listed the electoral district and the parish for that townland.

The census information recounted the family status on March 31, 1901. If there were visitors, boarders, or servants, they would have been included. Anyone who was at work or traveling on March 31 but returned the next day was counted, as long as they were not enumerated elsewhere.

The 1901 Census disclosed that my grandfather, James, was forty and his wife, Mary Anne, was thirty. Five children were listed: James (5), Maria (4), Patrick (2), Bernard (1), and John (3 months). James and Maria both attended school.

Since we could find no further information at the library, we turned to professionals for help. The South Mayo Family History Centre in Ballinrobe, like other history centers in Ireland, maintains a comprehensive database of civil and church records. They function as part of a network called the Irish Genealogical Project. Researchers there provided the baptism date for my grandparent's firstborn child, Belinda, who died a month after her birth in June of 1894. Also not included in the 1901 Census but listed in the database were Michael, baptized in January 1903, and my father Thomas, who was born in December 1904.

When the dates and facts from my preliminary search are combined with detailed information from the database and placed on a genogram, a picture of my Irish ancestors begins to materialize.

CONNECTING THE DOTS

Do you remember the thrill you had as a small child when you connected a page full of numbered dots and saw a picture emerge? This is what happens when you examine the data on your genogram. A picture of your ancestors comes to life as you connect the various bits of information you have gathered from different sources. With data from just one birth certificate, the 1901 census, and the South Mayo Family History Centre's computer database, I began to construct my family story.

My Irish grandmother, Mary Anne, who was born and raised in County Mayo, married a man who farmed acreage in the township of Devleash, a few miles from Kiltimagh. According to the database, Griffith's Valuation showed that James' father, Patrick, held 24 acres in common with five other tenants in 1856. (At the time of our visit, there were 14 acres in the family homestead.)

County Mayo was one of the poorest areas of Ireland. On our visit, we noticed that Devleash soil was rich in stones but poor in quality. The two-room stone house lacked both electricity and plumbing. Water was drawn from a well near the river quite a distance from the house, and peat for fuel had to be cut from a distant bog field and carried home.

The date of Mary Anne's wedding to James can be estimated at 1893, based on the birth date of their first child in 1894. Eight children, two girls and six boys, were born to James and Mary Anne during a period of ten years. Of those, seven survived. The firstborn, a girl, lived only one month.

The second child born to the young couple was named James. It is an Irish custom to name the firstborn male for his father. We know that Thomas was the last child born in the family because no other births were recorded after his.

Thomas did not know his grandfather, Patrick, who had lived with the family in the two-room house. According to the database, Patrick (61) died on January 26, 1901, three years prior to Thomas' birth. The elderly man's death occurred a month after John's birth, three weeks after his baptism, and two months before the 1901 census was taken. Imagine the stress and emotion that rocked that crowded cottage.

In 1905, less than four years later, my grandfather James died of consumption, the secondary phase of tuberculosis (also called phthisis). It was considered a "wasting disease" because of the slow-moving but debilitating symptoms, which included: fever, night sweats, weight loss, and fatigue. In the lungs, tuberculosis causes shortness of breath, a dry cough, blood and pus-filled sputum, and sometimes chest pain. Untreated, the disease is terminal. Ireland is damp and bitterly cold in winter, and the wind blows strong across the hilltop where my grandparents lived. One can imagine the difficulties this illness caused James, as he worked the farm and provided for his family's needs.

My father was ten months old when his father died, and his brother Michael's age was one year and nine months. James, the eldest living child, turned ten just one month after their father's death. As a widow with a brood of young children and no one to help her manage the farm after her husband's death, Mary Anne surely suffered hardship. James was too young to assume head-of-the-household responsibilities, though he probably tried. Less than three years after her husband's death, Mary Anne sold the house and property to a neighbor whose family still owns it. She packed up her children and a few belongings and left for the United States.

Your emigrant ancestors displayed similar courage and self-determination when they uprooted their families and set out for a distant land. Many left behind their worldly possessions and said goodbye to relatives they would never see again.

According to the ship's passenger records at the National Archives, Washington, D.C., Mary Anne and her children traveled to America as paid passengers, arriving at Boston in April, 1908. After clearing immigration, they proceeded to their destination in Springfield, Illinois, where three of Mary Anne's brothers worked in the coal mines.

From Springfield cemetery records and newspaper obituaries, I verified that within two months of their arrival in the United States, two of Mary Anne's children had died. Bernard, age eight, died in May. James, the eldest at twelve years ten months, died in June. Both children succumbed to complications from the measles. What a sad beginning for a widowed mother with hopes and dreams for a new and better life in America!

CELEBRATING FAMILY THROUGH STORY

In spite of unflattering stories I had heard about Mary Anne's stern and strong-willed personality, a different picture emerges from the genogram. With the ages, illnesses, and dates of death and immigration recorded on the chart, we can begin to surmise some of the particulars of Mary Anne's life between the time of her marriage in 1893 and her relocation to the United States in 1908.

When, in her mid-twenties, Mary Anne married a man ten years her elder, she probably believed that her future was secure. She would not have to worry about being a spinster. Since her husband managed his father's farm, there was also the prospect of financial independence. The loss of her first child was Mary Anne's introduction to grief. Yet even that must have been somewhat counterbalanced by joy when the couple was later blessed with a daughter and six sons, all healthy. Many Irish families of those times were less fortunate.

The Irish place tremendous value on family, and children of all ages were expected to help with the many farm and household chores. Mary Anne's sons would have been perceived as future providers, assuming responsibility for the farm and caring for their parents in old age. This would have bolstered Mary Anne's feelings of security. Sons also held the promise of perpetuating the family name, an important factor in most cultures.

The hard reality is that in a span of just twelve years, Mary Anne had married and given birth to eight children, and had already buried her firstborn child, her father-in-law, and her husband.

Given the fact that her husband died from a debilitating illness, it is reasonable to conclude that the harsh wet winters near the west coast of Ireland contributed to his demise. Life on that farm could not have been an easy existence for either James or Mary Anne.

In spite of all the hardships she endured, Mary Anne was generous. To a large family with few luxuries, a sewing machine represents wealth because it provides the means to make and repair clothing. Yet, we learned that Mary Anne gave her sewing machine to a relative before leaving Ireland. All that she took from Ireland were her memories and the few clothes, blankets, and linens she could carry.

Mary Anne showed spirit and courage when she sold the house and property where her husband's family had lived for more than 52 years. She sacrificed her only security in order to seek a better life abroad, using the 28£ she received from the sale of the farm to finance her trip.

Her decision to move to a foreign land may have been inspired by letters from her brothers abroad. Perhaps their hopeful stories of prosperity influenced her decision. Nevertheless, a farmer's wife, who had never ventured further than a mile or two from her home in the west of Ireland, needed a spirit of adventure to undertake such a daunting journey with her children.

First, they traveled by train across Ireland to the port of Queenstown (now Cobh). There, the young widow boarded a Cunard steamship with her seven young children, ages three to twelve, for the long journey across the Atlantic Ocean. My Aunt Marie (my father's sister) remembered feeling sick during most of the journey. A woman we spoke with at Cobh said that many emigrants waiting to sail from the port had no conception of the distance they would travel. Some, upon seeing a small outcropping of land in the harbor, would ask, "Is that America?"

As Mary Anne's story unfolds, we see her ongoing fortitude and tenacity. Within two months of her arrival in the States, she had already buried two more children. By her mid-thirties, she had known more grief in a few years than some people encounter in a lifetime. Her faith in God must have sustained her through her difficulties. How else can we account for her perseverance?

In spite of support from her brothers, reality quickly set in. Faced with medical and burial expenses for two children, and confronted with the need to support herself and her family in the "new world," Mary Anne placed her remaining five children in a Catholic orphanage nearly 100 miles away. If you are a parent, you can sympathize with her and the difficult choices she faced. She must have felt disillusioned. She certainly hadn't brought her family such a great distance with the intention of abandoning them.

"However long the road there comes a turning." This Irish saying seems to describe Mary Anne's philosophy. She must have clung to the hope and belief that life would improve. In the meantime, she continued plodding forward. She was not a quitter. My grandmother was forced to make tough decisions that deeply affected the lives of her children.

JUST IMAGINE

Imagine yourself as a child of Mary Anne. After losing your father to a devastating disease, you are uprooted from your home and brought to a distant country, leaving behind the close family and friends who were an integral part of your life. Within two months, two of your brothers die. Then, you and your siblings are placed in a Catholic orphanage a great distance from the town where your mother lives.

Can you visualize how you would feel in this situation? A lot depends upon your age and your temperament. The financial complications that led to your situation may be beyond the comprehension of a young child's mind. Even though your needs for food, clothing, shelter, and schooling are being met at the orphanage, you long for the comfort of your mother's love. You have feelings of separation, loss, and abandonment—emotions that find expression in anger. Perhaps you are ridiculed for your foreign accent and forced to sit in a corner of the classroom wearing a dunce cap. That happened to one of Mary Anne's sons.

Depending on your personality, your anger may be directed towards your mother, the strict sisters who care for you, or perhaps your father for dying and leaving you so vulnerable. You might project your anger towards God for allowing such hardships, and towards the orphanage and the church, which in a child's mind symbolize him.

Perhaps you have thoughts of running away. In your desire for attention, you may become the disruptive student, the class clown, or the school bully. Perhaps you internalize your anger and develop psychosomatic illnesses. These are some of the ways children strive for the attention and nurturing they crave.

A child of different temperament might view the orphanage as a warm and loving place. Such a response might result in the deep embrace of religion and spirituality in adulthood. That was the experience of a priest I know, who was led into his vocation through his experience of God's love in an orphanage.

How will the turbulent emotions of childhood be lived out in your adult life? Early experiences, both positive and negative, influence our relationship with God and with family. They also affect the choices we make as adults. Many people turn away from God because of a wounding early in life. Some people try to escape the pain of old wounds by numbing them with alcohol. For some, an entire lifetime is spent trying to fill a hole in the soul that craves love and validation as a human being who has worth.

Hopefully, you are beginning to comprehend how research into your family's history can breathe new life into your ancestors. You will recognize them as real flesh-and-blood people just like you, with strengths and weaknesses, hopes and dreams. You can begin to appreciate the qualities they passed on to you through the generations. Instead of blaming them for any weaknesses or failings, you may wonder, "What might I have done in their circumstances?"

With compassion for their difficulties and shortcomings, you can ask Jesus to grant them mercy and to bring them into the fullness of his redeeming love.

DEFINING YOUR TREE

Label this section of your notebook: *Family Data*.

1.   Assign a separate section in your notebook for each family grouping, and within that group a separate page for each member. Initially, you will work with four generations: you, your parents, your grandparents, and your great-grandparents. Separate entries will cover brothers and sisters, aunts and uncles, your spouse's family, and your children and grandchildren. First, concentrate on *your* immediate ancestors.

2.   Beginning with information on hand (dates of birth, death, marriage, children born), record each family member's data on the individual's page in your notebook.

3.   Expand your acquisition of vital statistics by searching for family birth certificates, marriage certificates, and death certificates. If you know the state and county, or country, in which your people were born, married, or died, and the approximate dates, you can obtain certified copies of these records.

4.   Check old family Bibles for records of family data.

5.   In your notes, include information about adoptions, illnesses, deaths, separations, divorces, and remarriages.

6.   Do you know of any serious accidents, suicides, miscarried babies, stillbirths, abortions, violent deaths, or acts of violence? Record these in your notebook.

Read: Is 43:1-7; Is 43:25; Is 44:3-4.

In promising redemption to Israel, God speaks also to us, the new Israel. We have been claimed by his Son Jesus, who suffered and rose from the dead to guarantee our place in heaven. This proof of the Father's unconditional love shows us how much he wants each one of us to stay close to him. He wants our presence, not only in this life, but for all eternity. Yahweh forgets our offenses and blots out our sins, blessing our descendants by an outpouring of his Spirit.

Become familiar with the symbols and abbreviations you can use to represent important elements in your family history. Understanding this shortcut language will help you develop your own genogram. (*see* Appendix I)

YAHWEH, FATHER-GOD

Yahweh, thank you for naming me as your child. Thank you, loving Father, for erasing my offenses and no longer remembering them. Please help me to erase from my mind any trace of resentment over the transgressions of my ancestors as I forgive them. Teach me to love as you love. You promised to reunite your people from the far corners of the earth, Lord. Assist me as I gather together my family members and bring them to your holy altar for healing. Your many blessings fill my heart with gratitude. Amen.

Chapter 4.

1.   Karl Rahner, "Biblical Homilies, 25." *Words of Faith* (NY: Crossroad),15.

2.   Michelle Healy, "Minus Marriage," *USA Today*, February 9, 2000, 6D.

3.   A certified copy of a birth certificate that includes the recorder's seal is recognized as a legal document for purposes of identification. Unlike certificates issued by hospitals, the certified copy contains details about the parents (age, occupation, and residence). It may include the mother's number of pregnancies and the number of live births.

5. CONSTRUCTING YOUR FAMILY'S STORY

"For a web begun God sends thread."
(French proverb)

Must you travel abroad in order to complete your family history search? Definitely not. You have already seen how civil and church records aid the family history search. These records are available to you no matter where you live. Certified copies can be ordered through the mail, and census reports are available on microfilm through genealogical libraries and the National Archives. (*see* Appendix II)

There are other avenues of investigation open to you, as well. Sources of genealogical information include numerous indexes and records available in books and on CD-ROMs, in addition to research opportunities through the Internet. Some immigration and ships' passenger records are indexed, but many are not. Without dates and places of departure or arrival, you will need perseverance to identify your ancestor among numerous others with the same name. Resources listed in Appendix II will help you get started.

Newspaper archives are a worthwhile source of information. Obituaries frequently include invaluable data such as dates and causes of death, residence of the deceased, former occupation, names of nearest kin, and date and location of funeral and burial. Articles about prominent people furnish considerable biographical details. One library I visited maintains a card index of newspaper obituaries and a complete collection of the city newspaper on microfilm.

A walk through family burial grounds can also yield new information. In a small cemetery, I found a headstone carved with my German great-grandfather's name, his Civil War Company, and his Infantry group. I almost missed the small stone. It was tucked behind a larger monument inscribed with both his and his wife's names.

While it was easy to trace his descendants from the date of his marriage forward, my mother's grandfather left no clues to his origins in Germany. Relatives have no recollection of his family or how he immigrated. The earliest mention of his name appears in an Illinois census when he was thirteen and living with a German blacksmith and his family. Civil War records in the National Archives yielded extensive details about his military service, medical records, health problems, pension application, and finally his death. That material alone provided insights into his character and to his need for healing prayer.

SPOKEN MEMORIES

In your enthusiasm for tracking down family information, don't overlook the obvious. Living relatives are one of your best resources for family history. Each person you interview may have only a small piece of the picture, which by itself can seem trivial. Added together, however, all the bits and pieces complete the story.

If relatives do not object, consider making an audio recording of your interviews with them. Freed from the distraction of taking notes, you can give careful thought to your questions, and can listen more attentively to the answers. I am often disappointed when I try to decipher notes that I hurriedly scribbled while people were speaking. Details get lost, along with the mood that prevailed at the time. A tape can be replayed and as you listen to the inflection of the voice, you will probably recall body language and facial expressions that accompanied the story.

There is an old saying that a picture is worth a thousand words. One man I know is videotaping conversations with his elderly relatives. He invites them to share about their memories and impressions, with the hope of building an oral family story he can share with future generations. Elderly relatives are usually delighted when we want to spend time with them and hear their stories. They have the leisure of time, and old memories return with a remarkable vividness in the golden years.

On a visit to Illinois, I drove my mother and her sister, both in their eighties, through the old neighborhoods where they grew up. It was fun to share their excitement as we passed houses where they had lived as children and saw schools they had attended. The incredible stories prompted by this excursion were captured on tape, in their own voices.

In addition to oral history, you may discover written family biographies. Perhaps someone kept a trip record, such as one my mother's German mother wrote when she visited Arizona during World War II. It includes comments on her automotive travels across the country, and reveals her poetic gift for description. The diary, which I received from a cousin after Grandma's death, was incomplete because pages had been torn out of the book. I may never know what family secrets she carried with her to the grave.

Recently, I received a copy of a brief family history, written in Grandma's familiar quavery handwriting. She describes the Illinois log house her father built with his own hands, and the 500-tree orchard he planted. A cabinetmaker and successful farmer, he was also a staunch Methodist and an advocate of the Prohibition Party. During his retirement years, he helped organize Sunday Schools throughout the state. I remember my grandmother sitting at the piano, singing and playing an old hymn, *The Church in the Wildwood*.[1] Reading her summary gave me deeper insights into her religious roots and what that song might have meant to her.

Diaries and letters are extremely valuable, as are documents such as: naturalization papers, wills, leases, deeds, maps, bills of sale, employment history, union cards, military records, drivers licenses, school records, yearbooks, diplomas, and awards.

Many of these treasures are just waiting to be discovered. They might be gathering dust in the attics and trunks of family elders because no one bothers to ask about them. Your questions may open new avenues of research.

WHAT IS MISSING IN THIS PICTURE?

Your request to view family photo albums can provide an easy and non-threatening way to launch your interview. When you inquire about old photos in the album, you will hear stories you otherwise might not have heard. As you examine photographs, pay close attention to family characteristics such as facial features and physical form. Observe body language, noticing any evidence of formality, informality, or even physical distance between people. In photos of family gatherings, notice who is absent as well as who is present. Why weren't the missing people in the picture? Where were they? These are the kinds of questions you must answer in order to know who in your family needs prayers, and why.

If you reach a roadblock in your interview, try volunteering an anecdote about your relative. You will discover that family members have different perceptions of the same events. Take note of all their stories. There are probably kernels of truth in each of them. It is all right to ask questions and point out discrepancies, but do so diplomatically.

Listen attentively. That which is left unsaid is often as important as that which is spoken. One the one hand, some people will be eager to share and even embellish their stories. Others may be reticent about saying anything that could be misconstrued as criticism. You are searching for the truth and your job is to sift all the data and prayerfully discern the truth.

When people tell you about your ancestor, ask about physical characteristics, personality traits, and temperament. Try to obtain a description of your ancestor's philosophy of life. What kind of reputation did your ancestor have? Were there any peculiarities or quirks? Eccentricities? What about nicknames? One distant relative in our family was called "King Cole" (after the nursery rhyme character) because he was considered mentally off-center.

Were there any family sayings that bear repeating? Any peculiar habits or obsessions? What can you learn about your relative's educational achievements? Professional accomplishments? Community involvement? Political activity or inactivity?

Did your ancestor have any significant wishes or dreams? Was there someone whose entire life was characterized by a dream of sailing around the world, or perhaps writing the great American novel? Were those ambitions fulfilled? If not, why not? How great was the ensuing disappointment?

As your personal family chronicles grow, you may find some glaring holes in your data. After I ran into dead-ends while researching Mary Anne, I discovered a library collection of the Springfield City Directory. The annual directories list the addresses of residents, along with their occupations and the names of other family members living with them. By combining information from these directories with my previous research, I was able to organize my data and understand it in terms of what else was going on at the time.

USING A TIMELINE

The chronology of events completed my research data and filled in some gaps in my family story. From the directories, I learned that Mary Anne lived with her relatives initially. After placing her children in the orphanage, she lived in various boarding houses where she worked to support herself.

In the 1910 Illinois census, my father's brothers and sister were cited as pupils at the orphanage, but five-year-old Thomas was listed as an inmate by the census taker. Inmate is a term that usually refers to a person confined to an asylum, a prison, or a poorhouse. It accurately describes my father's opinion of the place. Later in life, he bitterly recounted his memories of strict rules and the prison-like character of the orphanage.

Education of children is a top priority today. As you research your ancestors, keep in mind that in the early 1900s, harsh economic realities prevented many young people from finishing school. By determining your ancestor's educational level, you will learn about the family's financial circumstances.

From family stories, I know that none of Mary Anne's boys finished school. As soon as they were judged old enough to help support their mother, the three older boys left the orphanage to work on a farm for wages, room, and board. They must have felt affection for the owners who provided them with a home environment, because the farm's owner became a family friend. Photos in our family album document visits there years later, when I was a child.

Thomas, the youngest child, was the last to leave the detested orphanage that had been his home and prison for his first seven years in America. My father's citizenship documents show that in

January 1915, nearly seven years after arriving in the U.S., Mary Anne remarried. Her second husband, James, worked in the coal mines and lived in Mary Anne's neighborhood. From the city directory listings, I surmised that his wife had been dead less than a year when Mary Anne married him. Through this marriage, which occurred only four months after James became a U.S. citizen, Mary Anne and her children all became naturalized citizens.

Mary Anne was apparently an opportunist. Her marriage not only fulfilled her citizenship requirements, it enabled my father, Thomas, to leave the orphanage at age eleven and live with Mary Anne. My father remembered his stepfather, the only father he had ever known, as a cruel man with a serious drinking problem. Thomas must have wondered, at times, if home was really an improvement over the orphanage.

Court records show Mary Anne's divorce from James on October 12, 1916, less than two years after their marriage. First widowed and now divorced, Mary Anne moved frequently during the next several years. By following her trail through the annual city directories, I learned that Thomas is not listed with his mother from 1916 until 1919. He may have stayed with an uncle while Mary Anne sorted out her life once again.

My father's whereabouts during that period are a mystery. This gap in my family's history might have been prevented had I started the investigation before my father's death. It is never too soon to begin your family research.

From family interviews, I learned that Thomas' only sister left home soon after Mary Anne's marriage in 1915. Marie stayed with relatives for two years before moving to Chicago in 1918. Perhaps the tension at home was more than Marie and Thomas were willing to bear. Moving may have been their strategy for survival.

When Mary Anne purchased a house in 1918 with money from her sons' earnings, my father was finally reunited with his mother. By the seventh grade he had quit school to work at various jobs. After his death in 1991, I learned from his union that at the age of sixteen he was learning the printing trade at the city newspaper. This would become his life's occupation and his "university." An avid reader and a self-educated man, he quickly made up for his lack of formal education.

By working backwards, you can integrate your knowledge of an ancestor's personality traits with the facts you uncover. When you understand the obstacles and hardships that your ancestor overcame, you gain a deeper insight into the ways that events shaped your ancestor's life.

Little else is known about Mary Anne between 1908 and 1933, except that she endured more family grief. Her son Patrick was a passenger in an automobile that collided with a train shortly before his planned wedding in 1929. He died from his injuries a few days later, leaving behind his deeply saddened family and a grieving fiancée.

While I did not know Patrick, his portrait in the family album reveals a handsome man. The newspaper article describing his tragic death mentions his membership in the Knights of Columbus. This suggests that he was a committed Catholic who did not blame the Church for his earlier separation from his mother.

Patrick's sudden and tragic death at the age of thirty must have brought deep sorrow to the family, and especially to his mother. After the early deaths of Bernard and James, Patrick became the eldest son, with the attendant responsibilities. Also, his intended marriage held promise that he would father sons and continue the family name. Continuation of the family name is considered critical in many cultures.

WEAVING THE STORY

Family stories that are often repeated become the family legend. My family's stories helped fill in many details of our history. Three years after Pat's death, Thomas eloped with the woman he had been dating for seven years. The news that Thomas and Ruth were married on impulse by a justice of the peace angered Mary Anne. She insisted upon their remarriage by a priest the very next day. My father was twenty-seven, but still under his strong-willed mother's thumb. Even though he was angry about her reaction to his marriage, he complied with her demands for a church-recognized wedding.

It is probable that Mary Anne was not delighted with my father's choice of a wife. Even though my mother had converted to Catholicism, she was different from Mary Anne in many ways. My only photograph of my grandmother shows a plump and matronly Mary Anne. Her dark hair is pulled back in a bun and she wears a plain dark dress. One arm is thrown over the chair back and her facial expression seems to say, "Hurry up and get this over with!"

Contrast Mary Anne's demeanor and practicality with that of my attractive, blue-eyed, fashion-conscious mother whose taste always exceeded her budget. My earliest memories include our frequent trips to the beauty salon where Mother's blond hair was permed and styled and her nails were manicured. The temperaments of these two women must have put them on a collision course from the start.

At first, my parents tried living with Mary Anne but moved because my mother was unhappy there. By the time of my birth a year later, the upstairs rooms of Mary Anne's house had been converted to an apartment and a short time later we were living there again. My mother chose Ann for my middle name, an indication that she probably experienced ambivalent feelings towards this domineering but generous woman.

Around the time of my birth, Mary Anne's son John suffered a serious accident. While working in the railroad switching yard, his arm became caught between two freight cars and was completely severed.

Then, when I was only three months old, Mary Anne collapsed suddenly in my mother's arms. That night, my grandmother was pronounced dead in her bed. She died at age sixty-two of cholecystitis, a seriously infected gallbladder. The doctor who misdiagnosed her illness had also treated Patrick after his fatal automobile accident. A newspaper article reveals that initially there was hope for Pat's recovery, in spite of his badly lacerated leg and other injuries. However, he "gradually grew weaker until his death."

Perhaps Mary Anne's collapse triggered her sons' memories of the helplessness and rage they had felt while observing Patrick's demise and the doctor's incompetence. The priest who came to provide comfort and healing for Mary Anne and her family received their undeserved wrath instead of gratitude. Fearing their mother's impending death, my father and his brothers pulled the priest away from her bedside so that the doctor could save her. One can imagine the tension and turmoil surrounding Mary Anne's final hours.

Even though the cause of Mary Anne's death was listed as cholecystitis, I can't help wondering if she died of a broken heart. The many losses throughout her life must have dampened and diminished her hope. She had purchased a family plot for Patrick's burial, with gravesites for herself and her remaining children. The large headstone was engraved with the family name, since she no longer used the name of her second husband. The sadness of Mary Anne's many losses was shared by her children, as one after another, they saw the lives of their loved ones snuffed out. John followed Mary Anne to the grave at age thirty-five. Myocarditis, the infectious inflammation of his heart muscle, was attributed to the treatment he had received for his amputated arm two years earlier. The infection, which also caused John's beautiful reddish brown hair to fall out, resulted from a catgut stitch accidentally left in his flesh by the doctor.

A small photo of John, whose bald head is covered by a broad-brimmed hat, was trimmed by my father so that the armless shirtsleeve does not show. By cropping the photo, he may have attempted to isolate his feelings of sadness for his brother, feelings he never discussed. John suffered for a long time with a "heart cough" until his heart finally failed. One wonders if John had the same doctor as Mary Anne and Patrick.

Twelve years after Mary Anne's death, my father's only remaining brother died unexpectedly. While working in the San Francisco shipyards in 1945, Michael died suddenly. Notes in his file at the mortuary mention a recent scar of uncertain origin, caused by brain surgery or a mysterious head injury. His sister, Marie, arranged for his burial in the family plot. Marie died at age ninety and my father, the last survivor, died just before his eighty-seventh birthday. None of Mary Anne's sons married except my father. Marie had three daughters and I was my father's only child. There was no male heir to carry the family name.

Marie had many of the qualities that I associate with my grand-
mother. She was quick-witted, strong-willed, and fun to be with.
My father had Mary Anne's practicality and self-determination.
He was highly intelligent but his early life made him a skeptic.

HONORING MEMORY

Mary Anne's story illustrates some of the ways that you can
bring your ancestors to life. Family stories yield tremendous insights as you view your ancestors through the eyes and memories
of others who knew them, or knew of them.

From what I have learned in my research, I suspect that Mary
Anne had deep but simple faith. She appears to have lived by her
faith, upholding its principles for her family. From stories I have
heard, it is fair to say that her boys were not saints. Ruling with an
iron hand as she did, Mary Anne tried to guide her children along
the path she believed was right. They probably gave her a hard
time but even in adulthood, they knew better than to cross her. She
had presence and depth of conviction.

Because of her strength of character, Mary Anne could also be
formidable and difficult. However, she did not run away from challenges. She was a survivor. Mary Anne passed on her legacy of
survival to me, to my dad, and to his sister.

I'm grateful for her gifts of determination and tenacity in the
face of crisis, and for her special gift of storytelling. My father
often told me that I would have loved Mary Anne and her stories.
When I was two months old, my grandmother held me on her lap
at the table and fed me jelly from a spoon. I wish I could have
known Mary Anne.

Even more, I wish my father could have known her better too.
Mary Anne's desperate decision to place her three-year-old baby
in an orphanage was one my father could neither understand nor
forgive. Those long years of separation from his mother left him
deeply wounded.

Indirectly, Mary Anne passed the gift of faith to me. It was
because of my father's Catholicism that his future wife became a
convert. Her faithfulness to a religion she never fully understood

resulted in my religious education. Mother insisted upon it, even though my father bore a lifelong anger toward the Church. His resentment was a direct result of his early separation from his mother and his rebellion against the strict sisters who had raised him.

My father's faith-crisis was the subject of my prayers from early childhood. I recall a time late in his life when he said, "I wish I had your faith." Silently, I prayed, "You heard him, Lord. Give him the faith he is asking for." My prayers were answered. He experienced a deep healing of his anger and I saw his gentle spirit emerge from beneath the layers of hurt he had carried since childhood.

My prayers during Masses for my family tree have asked for healing of all the losses and grief experienced by this branch of my family. I have prayed about their pain and separation, their misunderstandings and grievances. I apologized to God for the behavior of Mary Anne's sons, who in a state of panic forcefully ushered away the priest who brought God's peace and final blessing to her deathbed. Even though our Father in heaven knows their hearts, I felt it was important to prayerfully voice the apology they may not have verbalized during their lives.

As you research the past, ask yourself how your ancestors handled death. In what ways did your family pass down a religious heritage? Can you attribute your own faith and beliefs to your ancestors? How have you been influenced by their religious tenets or lack of them? Scripture tells us to pass down God's word to each generation, so that our children will place their confidence in God and keep his commandments. (Ps 78:1-8)

If faith is part of your legacy from your ancestors, you have ample reason to be thankful. The gift of faith outlasts anything material that we might value. If, however, faith and godliness were not woven into the fabric of your ancestors' lives, this will guide your prayers for family healing. You can ask God to forgive their ignorance of his love and to reward them now with the blessings that were missing in their earthly lives.

Because I believe in the love and mercy of God, I also believe that my father has been reunited with his mother, with the father he never knew, and with his sisters and brothers. I pray for their reconciliation with a cruel and wounded stepfather. In the company of Jesus and the Father, they now enjoy the true meaning of family. I pray that they laugh and tell stories and sing with the angels. Jesus promised:

> I am the resurrection and the life. If anyone believes in me, even though he dies he will live, and whoever lives and believes in me will never die. (Jn 11:25-26)

READING BETWEEN THE LINES

Label this section of your notebook *Family Interviews*. Before you begin this section, pray for divine guidance, wisdom, and discernment. As you prepare for family healing, you need good intuition and keen insights. These gifts are readily available from the Holy Spirit.

1.   Make inquiries among family members. Perhaps someone has already compiled a genealogy.

2.   A wealth of details and insights can be garnered from written or oral biographies, medical histories, diaries, and old letters.

3.   Look at family photo albums. Observe body language for clues. How do family members relate to one another? Who is missing from pictures and why?

4.   Note family moves. Did any family members relocate from one country to another? Who moved? Who was left behind? Who was deeply missed?

5.   Referring to the notes and/or tapes of your interviews with family members, try to summarize what you have learned.

6.   Make a list of any unanswered questions that require further research.

7.   What can you determine about your ancestors based on the facts and stories you have gathered?

8.   What implications can be drawn from the stories told? What was not said may be as important what was said.

9.   Were family stories about relatives flattering or unflattering? Do they ring true?

10.   Did you verify statements made by your sources? Different family members may have different perceptions of people and events. By comparing their stories, you can begin to separate truth from fiction.

Your objective is to gain a better understanding of your ancestors. As patterns emerge on your genogram, you will notice connections that previously were not apparent.

SHINE YOUR LIGHT OF TRUTH, LORD

Come Holy Spirit, and grace me with the gift of discernment. As I research my family history and probe for unhealed wounds and brokenness, I rely on your guidance. Keep me always on the path of truth and love, for without these my research and prayers have no value. Bless me with the joy of finding good attributes in my ancestors. Grant me a thankful heart for the inherited virtues that have positively shaped my life, and a forgiving heart for any ancestral failings that have become stumbling blocks for me and for my family. Amen.

Chapter 5.

1. Dr. William S. Pitts, composer.

6. RELATIONSHIPS

"No man is an island, entire of itself..."
(John Donne)

Just as a tree is at home surrounded by other trees, people through-out the ages have tended to cluster together in community. In choosing home sites, early settlers sought areas with a good water supply, fertile lands, and easy accessibility. Gradually, structured communities evolved out of the needs of people for government, religious worship, staples and supplies, and a burial place. As a result, villages had at their center a church, a school, a post office, a jail, and a cemetery, as well as the services of a general store, a blacksmith and other tradespeople.

Suburban homes are still clustered near shopping centers, schools, and transportation corridors. Today, however, it is pos-sible to live in a city surrounded by hundreds of other people with-out even knowing the next-door neighbors. Many people of our time take extreme measures to protect their privacy and they are proud of their independence.

Such was not the case in times past, when neighbors comprised an extended family. They were there to help, whatever the prob-lem. You might borrow a cup of sugar this week. They might borrow from you next week. They would help with your barn rais-ing, bring a meal when someone died, and help you quell the flames if your barn caught fire. You would do likewise. Neighbors pro-vided an informal support system for one another.

Unlike many of today's mobile and uprooted families, earlier generations were more likely to put down roots in one place and stay put. Unless they had a compelling reason to relocate, your parents or grandparents probably lived in the same area their entire lives. The fact that many generations of a family often lived and died in the same town is readily apparent when you read old grave markers in town cemeteries.

EXPANDING THE BOUNDARIES

Since family healing is the main objective of your research, your investigation takes you beyond the dates and places of births and deaths. You are seeking patterns of illness, of harmful attitudes, of brokenness, and other destructive behavior that may have contributed to current family problems. As your data expands and you continue to record notations on your genogram, you will begin to recognize connections between the problems of ancestors and those of living family members.

Your inquiry into family history can extend outside the boundaries of blood relatives. In many cases, friends and neighbors may have become an extension of your family. Godparents, attendants at weddings, Confirmation sponsors, and pallbearers probably had close ties to your family. These are usually chosen from the immediate circle of friends. While these are not considered official branches of the tree for genealogy purposes, they are potentially useful sources of information because they were involved with your family during significant life events.

Family friends and neighbors may shed new light on old family mysteries. For instance, in the case of private matters such as adoptions, an old family friend may know details that you could not learn through library and archival research. In our family, when an elderly godparent disclosed a family secret she had concealed since the 1930s, she appeared relieved to end her many years of silence. Furthermore, her valuable inputs informed and guided my prayers for family healing.

From their vantage point on the periphery of your family, friends sometimes offer a fresh perspective and greater objectivity than that found among immediate family members. In your eagerness to complete your research, don't disregard the clues they provide. Their insights may illuminate your investigation.

THE GARDEN OF FRIENDSHIP

There is wisdom in the old saying, "Tell me who your friends are and I'll tell you who you are." People usually seek companionship with others who share similar likes and interests. While we cannot choose our ancestors, most people can and do choose the friends with whom they will share time and confidences.

True friendship involves commitment to another person and deep friendships are marked by empathy and caring. In such a relationship, we might confide that which we would never disclose to a relative or a casual acquaintance.

Since friendship implies a bond of affection, trust, and loyalty, deep hurt results when that trust is violated. Depending on the seriousness of the breech and the wounded person's unwillingness to forgive, a relationship might be irreparably severed. As you investigate your ancestor's life, note any enduring friendships, broken relationships, or the absence of friends. These associations provide insights into your relative's personality. Any lack of forgiveness or antisocial behavior indicates a need for healing prayer. Beyond immediate family and friends, the neighborhood plays a positive or negative role in shaping a person's life. A neighborhood is more than a cluster of houses, just as a forest is more than a stand of trees. Both are characterized by undercurrents of life and transfers of energy that are not apparent to the casual observer. The word neighbor originated from ancient words meaning "near dweller" and neighborhood represents neighbors who share specific characteristics.

People select the neighborhoods in which they live and raise their families, just as they choose friends. Water always seeks its own level and the choice of a neighborhood is a good indicator of lifestyle, economics, and social status.

When neighborhoods were smaller and lives were more closely linked, people not only knew their neighbors, they knew each other's personal business as well. Neighbors could be your best friends, as well as your worst enemies. A lot of information that passed over the garden fence was disseminated as gossip in the local village. This is still the case in small communities.

If you have played the game of telegraph, you know that the words in a sentence quickly become distorted when they are passed in whispers around a circle. In a similar way, statements can take on a different shape and meaning as they are reiterated between family members, neighbors, or friends. Innocent statements are sometimes misinterpreted.

DIFFICULT RELATIONSHIPS

Our ancestors did not have the benefit of the myriad self-help books and resources that are available today. In order for you to better understand their faults and weaknesses, it helps to know a little about psychology.

Good communication is essential in all relationships. Proper education in communication helps a lot in the prevention of domestic arguments, neighborhood squabbles, and employment disputes. Many people reach adulthood without mastering basic communication skills, and people with inadequate communication skills are likely to experience relationship problems. Parents with poor conversational abilities pass on these traits to their children, since they cannot effectively teach what they do not know.

You may have a relative who can never make a decision. When you ask which movie or restaurant they prefer, they answer, "I don't know. You decide." Later, they may complain about your choice, causing you to feel frustrated because you were unable to anticipate their expectations.

Some people use manipulative behavior to express their needs and desires. Every time you cooperate, you feel "set-up" and exploited. Your reaction is honest because manipulative behavior is very controlling; however, you need to explore your own participation in the role of victim. Often, the victim is guilty of self-defeating behavior because he sets himself up to be victimized. These patterns are learned early in life.

If you come away from family encounters gritting your teeth, tearing your hair, and feeling put-upon, take comfort in knowing you are not alone. These kinds of problems are so prevalent, entire books have been written on how to overcome them. Effective communication is a learned behavior and the lack of it may be an acquired or inherited behavior pattern in your family. Take heart; it is never too late to learn proper assertiveness.

My children taught me a lot about assertive language. I recall asking my teenagers, "Would you like to take out the trash?" You can guess their response. Then I learned to say, "Take out the trash, please." They still didn't want to, but they cooperated because my directions were clear and left no doubt about my expectations.

My poor communication skills resulted from my desire to please everyone around me, and from my willingness to feel guilty. Finally, a wise counselor recommended a book that helped change my thinking. With concentrated effort, I learned new ways of communicating my wishes. Old habits are difficult to overcome but they can be conquered. If I find myself backsliding, I return to the book for a refresher course.

Assertiveness should not be confused with aggression. In order to get their way, two-year-olds throw tantrums, while schoolyard bullies threaten violence. On the other hand, properly assertive people know what they want and use words that clearly and inoffensively state their requests. By their honest communication, they avoid sending mixed and confusing signals. Manuel J. Smith's book, *When I Say No, I Feel Guilty,* teaches methods for eliminating roadblocks to clear and honest communication.

Manipulation is one tactic used by people who have not learned to express themselves assertively. Perhaps someone has you jumping through hoops. No matter how often or how high you jump, it is never enough. According to Dr. Wayne W. Dyer in *Pulling Your Own Strings*, being free from victimization includes maintaining a positive attitude, recognizing your own capabilities, and teaching others how to treat you. People cannot victimize you unless you allow them to. Your refusal to play the game causes their behavior to change accordingly. Dr. Dyer's book details healthy strategies to help you improve relationships and assume control over your life.

Psychologists say that those mannerisms of others that drive us bonkers are frequently traits we harbor within ourselves. Your strong reaction to the faults of another calls for inward reflection. What is it about a person that sets you off? Are you guilty of the same traits? By recognizing your own weaknesses and working to correct them, you can improve your relationship with others.

Honest communication between family members helps to relieve tension and that begins with you. In addition to healing present relationships, you have the opportunity to pass down healthy communication skills to your offspring. Meanwhile, as you better understand similar inadequacies in your ancestors, you will be moved with compassion to forgive any legacy of family problems caused by their weaknesses.

FUSSING AND FEUDING

Major disagreements frequently evolve out of simple misunderstandings. When we misinterpret the words or actions of another, we may react with hurt feelings and anger. It is not uncommon for people to overreact in such a situation. Quarrels that remain unresolved can lead to long-term enmity and feuding that is passed down through the family. People learn what is modeled for them, whether it is love or hate, and attitudes of intolerance become part of the personality. They endure and expand. However, when prejudice is questioned and illuminated under the light of love, truth, and reason, a change of heart can occur.

In Shakespeare's *Romeo and Juliet*, it took the tragic deaths of the youthful lovers to finally end the longstanding conflict between their families. An American counterpart is the infamous feuding of the Hatfields and McCoys. This true story of hatred between clans and love between a young couple resulted in senseless and lamentable deaths before the spirit of hatred and revenge was played out.[1]

Feuding among relatives is devastating to the family structure and painful for all. Human beings share a gift of language that other creatures lack. Isn't it ironic that our precious gift of words—which enables us to sing praises to God and to encourage and affirm others—can defame another's character, can turn us against one another, and can destroy morale in the family and elsewhere?

Feuding in the family occurs in degrees. It may be subtle in critical remarks, teasing, and practical jokes. It is more evident in rudeness, slander, lies, and spitefulness. When feuding escalates and family members align with one side or the other, a major fracture in the family structure results.

While family feuding might appear to be an isolated case of sustained anger, research of the family's history often reveals a pattern of this behavior down through the generations. Perhaps within your family the intolerance has become so intense that certain family members no longer speak to each other. They may even disavow their blood relationship.

AN OUNCE OF PREVENTION

Even as you research the past for indications of feuding, don't overlook the present. Take note of your current family relationships and interactions. A lot can be done in the present moment to prevent future breakdowns in your family's communication.

Feelings of hostility that arise in adulthood can have their origin in the sibling rivalry of childhood. Children naturally seek attention and love from their parents. Each one wants to be the favorite. Even the most skillful parenting may not prevent children from feeling displaced and unloved when a new baby, or a new stepparent, arrives on the scene.

A child's perception is not always the reality. No matter how much a child is loved, he may not perceive that love. Serious problems evolve from comments such as: "Why can't you be like your brother?" or "Why don't you get good grades like your sister?" The perception that another sibling is loved more nurtures feelings of jealousy. Healthy attitudes of competition can become warped. A child's belief that he is inferior contributes to low self-esteem and to the distorted thinking that leads to family feuding.

Grandparents and other family members can help facilitate the healing of wounded self-esteem by supporting parents' efforts to build their children's self-confidence. Dr. Lillian Carson stresses the grandparents' important role of guiding children by their good example.[2] Their willingness to listen and affirm makes a tremendous difference to children.

Statistics support the idea that "grandparents have a strong presence and influence in all of American family life." Research at the University of Massachusetts found that among people over 55, 76% spend an average of 13.6 hours a week in contact and caregiving with grandchildren and great-grandchildren. Bela Bognar, a professor at Wright State University, credits his grandparents with teaching him religious, family, and human values during communist oppression in Hungary. Commenting on the propaganda that was broadcast daily at his Budapest high school, he said, "...we laughed at the propaganda; our grandmothers taught us other things, and that's what we believed."[3]

Many grandparents are helping to raise their children's children. Some are assisting with childcare while both parents work. Others have become the primary caregivers for grandchildren whose parents are either dysfunctional, divorced, or in some other way incapacitated. For these families, ancestral healing is indicated to break any destructive patterns responsible for the broken homes.

On the other end of the scale, many parents find themselves sandwiched between two needy generations. While attempting to provide for their children's upbringing and education, they are also challenged by the responsibility of caring for elderly and infirm parents. Many family disputes erupt over these situations.

If the role of caring for elderly parents falls on just one dutiful family member, that person may experience feelings of alienation and/or martyrdom, as well as anger and self-righteousness. In ideal situations, siblings find a way to work together and support one another's efforts. With careful planning and teamwork, hurtful disagreements can be prevented.

Open discussions and advanced planning can prevent a lot of problems. My own parents found discussions about future infirmity or death uncomfortable. As a result, my husband and I were forced to make very difficult decisions on their behalf, when they were no longer able to do so. With better foresight and gentle assertiveness, I might have persuaded them to talk things over with me just once.

A lot of family stress is avoided when aging parents can be encouraged to make long-term plans before there is a need. It is wise to consider financial arrangements as well as the possibility of serious illness *before* problems arise.

It is a loving gesture to provide relatives with guidance about your own preferences. Estate planning and a living will (also called an Advance Directive or Durable Power of Attorney for Healthcare) insure that a person's final wishes are respected.

A new and different trend that arose in the 1990s found siblings battling one another for the privilege of caring for an elderly parent. This conflict is not born of love and altruism, however, but out of greed for the family inheritance. Squabbles over family money and property are not new, but this type of custody struggle puts a different wrinkle on an old situation.

Whether or not a family feud has roots in earlier generations, the danger of passing on this divisive tendency to future generations is serious. Any pattern of family feuding is reason enough to have prayer for family healing. As you gather family history, you will encounter varying levels of woundedness and family grievances.

You may be the one person who is called by God to initiate his healing within your family. As God's emissary, you have the opportunity to help mediate differences and to remedy family defects. Through your prayers for generational healing, your family tree will be strengthened and renewed.

EXPLORING THE OLD NEIGHBORHOOD

Label this section of your notebook: ***The Neighborhood***. By researching the community in which ancestors lived, you gain insights into their cultural background and activities.

1.   Was your relative popular among peers?   School yearbooks often contain comments from friends and teachers.   The absence of comments is also revealing.   If you do not have access to family members' yearbooks, check school archives and the shelves of the community library.   Note your relative's participation, or lack of it, in school government, athletics, drama group, the arts.   Yearbooks mention notable achievement and predictions about who is most likely to succeed.

2.   The National Archives has military service records dating from 1775 into the 20th Century.   These records may describe rank and company, battle injuries, reasons for absence from roll call, and medical details described in pension applications.

3.   Old community newspapers in historical archives and libraries are resources for news about marriages, births, sicknesses and deaths.   Human interest stories about local residents reveal their politics, social events, misfortunes, crimes, financial disasters, and embarrassments. Check old metropolitan newspapers for local news as well as regional, national, and world news of wars, political strife, natural disasters, and economic trends (recession, depression, or boom times) that impacted your ancestor's lives.

4.   Regional attitudes, which are as varied as regional dialects, are important.   Be alert for patterns of superstition and prejudice. Cultural traditions and beliefs influence family attitudes.

5.   Search regional libraries for recorded wills, leases, deeds, and bills of sale. Historical societies may have helpful indexes that can be searched by family name and location.

6.   Plat maps can help you locate your ancestor's residence, even though the area has since undergone growth and change.

THE WORLD IS A GARDEN OF NEIGHBORHOODS

Lord, help me to appreciate my significance in the universe. At times, I think that my interests are the only ones that matter and my concern becomes narrowly focused on my family's needs and happiness. Help me recognize my connection to others throughout the world. Your great commandment calls me to love all of my neighbors, no matter how different they may seem to me. As I pray for family peace and healing, let my small efforts be a step toward peace throughout the whole earth. Unite all of your children, Lord, through the power of your love. Amen.

Chapter 6.

1. "America's Biggest Feud" by V. C. Jones. In *People's Almanac 2*, David Wallichinsky and Irving Wallace (NY: William Morrow & Company, Inc., 1978), 32-36.

2. Dr. Lillian Carson, *The Essential Grandparent: A Guide to Making a Difference* (FL: Health Communications, Inc. 1996), 44.

3. Bernard Starr, "East or West, granny power is fundamental," Scripps Howard News Service. In *Los Angeles Times*, April 21, 1998, A10.

7. THE PAST INFORMS THE PRESENT

*"As generations come and go,
Their arts, their customs, ebb and flow."*[1]

Family was first blessed when God created Adam and Eve and told them to be fruitful and multiply. Later, the Father reaffirmed the value of the family matrix by sending his Redeemer Son to us as an infant. Jesus was born into a human family and he grew up within a community of neighbors. Knowing a little about the framework of society in the time of Jesus gives us insights into the story of his life. People of his time, like any other, were influenced by the rules and customs that shaped their communities.

God's Chosen People of Israel exhibited strong national pride and a reverence for family ties. Among their many customs, the choosing of a child's name was an important decision because the name was associated with a person's character. We also know from Scripture that they honored their family genealogies.

In most societies, choosing a name for the baby is still an important decision. It is common practice to name the firstborn son after the father and in some countries, certain rights, endowments, and responsibilities adhere to the oldest son. You will probably find reoccurring names in your family's lineage.

National pride is a relevant factor in every culture. Early immigrants to America found comfort in sharing culture with people like themselves. By settling into ethnic neighborhoods and maintaining old world traditions, they eased their transition into the culture of the new world. This practice is still popular with immigrants today, though family tension rises when younger generations assimilate into the American culture more quickly than their parents. What outside influences contributed to your ancestor's lifestyles and habits? As you investigate your genealogy, you need to be aware of their cultural environment, in addition to any difficulties surrounding their lives. It is also helpful to understand how social change impacted your predecessors.

TECHNOLOGY—FRIEND OR FOE?

Technology escalated so rapidly in the 20th Century, it is easy to forget that what we consider the norm today was not the norm for previous generations. However, with research and a little imagination you can envision the ways your ancestor's lives were affected by their living conditions, and by social, economic, and political issues of their individual eras.

My mother (1909-1997) kept pace with technology through nine decades of dramatic sociological change. As a child she rode in a horse and buggy, used an outhouse, pumped water from the well, and helped sell vegetables from her father's garden. She drove an automobile as a young adult, washed clothes in a wringer-type washing machine in her 20s, and helped build fighter aircraft in her 30s.

As a supermarket grocery checker in her 40s and late 50s, she had progressed from the coal-burning stove to the microwave oven, from the wireless to cable TV, and from the buggy to jet travel. She adapted. Had her eyesight been better in her 80s, she would have become computer-literate and explored the Internet. Your ancestors made similar adjustments through a century of rapid and dramatic changes.

The same technology that is considered progress by some may be cursed by those whose jobs become obsolete. Computer chips and robots have already displaced many from their jobs as smart machines do the work of many. Advancing technology demands that you either "keep up or fall out."

How much different would your life be today without discoveries such as penicillin, first used on humans in the winter of 1940-41? Perhaps you have ancestors, as I do, who could have lived longer with the benefit of antibiotics or better diagnostic techniques.

The X-ray was in use for medical diagnosis just a few years after its discovery in 1895. However, the CT scanner did not come into general use until the late 1970s. Thanks to technology of the 1970s and 1980s, the thick eyeglasses once required after cataract surgery have been replaced by miniature lens implants.

Surgeries that once required lengthy and expensive hospitalization have become routine outpatient procedures, thanks to microsurgery. We benefit from wonder drugs, artificial hips and knees, heart valves and organ transplants, while scientists research cures for cancer, heart disease, AIDS, and other life-threatening diseases. Just as medical advances have extended life, social reforms have contributed to the quality of life

CHANGE IN THE WORKPLACE

As early as the 1800s, trade unions were organizing workers in a common fight for improved working conditions, fringe benefits, free public education, the abolishment of the debtors' prison, and a unified voice for the common laborer. Those early reforms aided your ancestors and indirectly benefited your own lifestyle.

Many of the injustices suffered by workers have aroused deep passions. Strikes against management have been known to erupt in violence. Did major strikes affect your ancestor's ability to support the family? Was your relative involved in violent protests? Vast social and economic changes have also resulted from the invention of the digital computer in the 1940s and the advent of the silicon chip in the 1970s. As new jobs were created through the computerization of industry, old jobs became obsolete.

Just as your ancestors were affected by earlier trends, you are living through times of incredible change that will impact future generations. New business philosophies in the 1990s resulted in the career-breaking displacement of many in middle management positions, at a time when corporations were posting huge profits. When their skills were no longer needed, many workers were forced into premature retirement.

Downsizing, a job-reduction trend that began in the 90s, has significant social implications for younger generations too. Savings for college dwindle as affected families struggle to support basic family needs. Meanwhile, new doors of opportunity open for some college graduates, who are welcomed by industry at salaries lower than those they displaced. This trend continues in the new millennium, which is also witnessing the failure of numerous dot.com companies. Such economic trends eventually affect all generations.

From the horse-drawn buggy to the automobile, and from the first successful airplane flight to supersonic aircraft and space shuttles, moon landings, and Mars explorations, the modernization of transportation has changed the way people work and live. Today's progress drives the future.

In today's fast-paced society, the insatiable desire for instant information and communication fuels technology. In less than 150 years, we have progressed from the Pony Express and the hand-cranked telephone to cellular phones, pagers, faxes, palm-sized computers, and e-mail. News that once was exchanged at the general store is now transmitted worldwide by satellite. All of these innovations impact the way your family lives and works, while family togetherness competes with the intrusion of the Internet and other media attractions.

WHEN ELEPHANTS FIGHT, THE GRASS IS TRAMPLED

In addition to revolutionary advances in communication, industry, labor laws, and medical science, people born early in the 20th Century witnessed major wars. War changes the fabric of society while stimulating technological research and inventions. One example is the progression from biplanes, battleships, machine guns, submarines, and chemical warfare in World War I (1914-1918) to the wholesale destruction wrought in 1945 by the atomic bomb, which ended World War II.

Think about how many lives were lost or changed by the events of these and other conflicts. How was your family affected by these wars? Someone in your family may have built, or considered building, a shelter from radioactive fallout during the escalation of nuclear war threats in the 1960s. Balanced against the desire to preserve the family and protect them from the effects of a nuclear bomb was the ethical realization that neighbors would have to be excluded.

In every war, regardless of which country is declared winner, everyone loses. People lose their loved ones, their health, their homes, and their family cohesion. The economic burden of war is devastating. Even worse, the human spirit is deeply wounded when nations wreak havoc and destruction upon each other in the name of peace.

Your family history has been scarred in some way by war. Explore the possibility that among your ancestors there were war heroes and/or seriously wounded veterans. Perhaps your ancestors include commanding officers whose consciences were burdened by decisions they made in the battlefield. People who serve in the military can suffer mental distress long after a war has ended. Haunted by memories and tormented by nightmares, they find recovery difficult.

Such veterans of World War I were said to be suffering from shell shock. Some were accused of being cowards because their disorder was misunderstood. There was a high incidence of post-traumatic stress disorder among Vietnam vets, whose minds and souls recoiled at witnessing or participating in the inhumanity of that war.

Were any of your family members missing in action or detained in concentration camps as prisoners of war? Did anyone suffer from war-related mental or physical disability?

There are conscientious objectors, draft dodgers, dissenters, and deserters in every war. How was your family affected by the Korean conflict of the 1950s? By America's involvement in the Vietnam War during the 1960s and 1970s? Were generations of your family divided by their opposing convictions about involvement in these conflicts?

Unlike war, in which the enemy is openly hostile, terrorism is covert. It aims, by instilling fear, to virtually paralyze its intended victims. The 20th Century witnessed isolated incidents of terrorism around the world that claimed the lives of military personnel and civilians. Such sudden and unexpected loss of even one life to violence is tragic and wounds our sensibilities. When thousands of lives were lost in the September 11, 2001 terrorist attacks on the World Trade Center and the Pentagon in the U.S., citizens recoiled with intense anger and disbelief over the scope and magnitude of the crimes. Hardly a survivor's life was untouched by the nearness of the trauma. Then, as the nation mourned the overwhelming human loss from the attacks, an outbreak of random bioterrorism added to the menacing grotesque face hiding behind the vicious attacks.

As news reporters struggled for language to describe the shocking events as they unfolded, historians were wondering how present and future generations would be impacted. This was clearly a pivotal point in the history of the United States, one that touched countries throughout the world.

Patriotism resurfaced in the wake of the terrorist attacks, along with a sense of vulnerability and a change in priorities for many Americans. Airlines, theme parks, and department stores, along with the stock market, were the first to reflect the resulting impact on the economy. As you work on your family healing, you must also consider and pray about the ways these events have affected your family.

SOCIAL CHANGE AND THE FAMILY

Laws result in the reorganization of society, and the political results of these changes trickle down to future generations. Many laws are aimed at the equalization of freedom and benefits, and affect the distribution of public funds for health, welfare, and education. One of the most-noticed and painful effects is felt in the bank account. The taxes which fund such benefits pit the "haves" against the "have-nots." Disagreements about who should pay for education, medical care, and entitlements create adversarial relationships between the generations. This was as true yesterday as it is today.

The 1929 stock market crash plunged the United States into the Great Depression that lasted into the 1940s. Banks failed, businesses were ruined, and millions who lost their jobs were reduced to poverty. Encampments of the poor and homeless were numerous. After his 1932 election to the presidency, Franklin D. Roosevelt enacted the New Deal program to help the country rebound from the Depression.

The New Deal included the formation of programs to employ the jobless. The Works Progress Administration (WPA), which employed people to work on government construction projects, provided the means for my maternal grandfather to support his family as an electrician. Many were also employed through the Tennessee Valley Authority (TVA), which developed flood control projects and built dams and hydroelectric power stations. Similar programs provided work for writers and actors.

The Social Security Act of 1935 paved the way for humanitarian benefits that have made a significant difference in the lives of the elderly, widows, the poor, and many with disabilities. In your research, consider how your own family was affected. With the growing number of elderly people in America's population, new laws will impact the financial security of the elderly in the future.

Is there a pattern of unemployment, welfare assistance, or disability in your family? In addition to economic trends, look for other underlying problems such as poor health, lack of education, broken families, illegitimate pregnancies, foster care, and similar conditions which also may be inherent in your family and require your prayers. Perhaps there is a pattern of poor business management or an absence of good judgment in managing finances.

VOICES OF THE PEOPLE

Civil liberties, which are guaranteed by the United States Constitution, have required persistent efforts on the part of minority groups to ensure that those rights exist for all citizens. When individuals band together for a common cause, the voice of the people is heard through their political activism. However, the price of activism is often great and frequently involves bloodshed.

While prejudice of any type might have roots in an actual event, the attitude is often kept alive long after the incident that first aroused it. Such opinions are passed down from one generation to the next. We may be guilty of accepting without question the negative attitudes we learned as children. One subtle way that prejudice imbeds its tentacles is through verbal slurs and disrespect for other ethnic, racial, and religious groups. In spite of laws and activism aimed at reversing prejudice, it still exists today. Your prayers for healing your family line can ask for the eradication of intolerance within your family.

Slavery, the demeaning practice of "owning" persons in violation of their human rights, has existed in every known society. The Bible contains many references to slaves, and archeologists have found evidence of this practice as early as 2000 BC. Slavery was in existence in Europe long before Columbus discovered America. In the United States, the importation of Africans by traders began in 1619 when a Dutch frigate landed at Jamestown and exchanged the cargo of Africans for supplies. By 1860, the slave population in America exceeded 3 million.[2]

Tribes in Africa were known to raid neighboring villages and sell their captives to slave traders' ships. Were any of your relatives slave traders or slave holders? According to the 1860 slave schedule for Arkansas, slaves were owned by both whites and Native American Indians, as well as by people of mixed blood. One slave owner in the Creek nation was designated as a Negro.[3] The practice of slave breeding occurred in Virginia and other states. Some slave owners were benevolent and kind, while others degraded slaves and treated them cruelly.

Were any of your ancestors slaves? Were they mistreated? Does racial bias or intolerance exist in your family today? Have family members belonged to the Ku Klux Klan, Nazi or Neo-Nazi organizations, Black Panthers, or other militant groups? Is there a prevailing attitude of hatred or revenge in your family?

Perhaps your grandmother or great-grandmother joined in the lengthy battle for women's suffrage in the United States. The suffragette movement was first organized in the mid-1800s, but it was not until the 1920 ratification of the Nineteenth Amendment that American women were guaranteed the right to vote. The ongoing struggle of working women to receive equal pay and recognition is not new. Susan B. Anthony was actively addressing this issue in 1869.

Within your family, do men and women receive equal respect? Men have long been accused of macho tendencies and women have countered by ridiculing and mocking men. Such attitudes on either part are demeaning and divisive. They tear at the moral fabric of the family and they send the wrong message to children. We are all equal in God's sight. Each one is a beloved child of God. Do you teach your children respect? Do you allow them to watch television programs that distort and demean the dignity of men and women?

Did your ancestors inherit or pass on attitudes of religious bias? Do erroneous beliefs persist in your family today? It is a contradiction to denigrate the beliefs of others while claiming to profess a faith that embraces God's love for all of his children. Our prayers for unity can help foster an end to division and feuding among God's family.

Discrimination and bigotry of any kind are contrary to the two great commandments of Jesus. (Mk 12:29-31) Through his life, his actions, and his death and resurrection, Jesus showed us how to love our neighbors. He also gave us the story of the Good Samaritan, who ministered with compassion to a dying stranger when others had passed him by. The Samaritan went the extra mile for the injured man, proving himself a good neighbor. Jesus tells us, "Go, and do the same yourself." (Lk 10:37)

The teachings of Jesus bid us to do more than tolerate our neighbor. We are to love with the love of Christ. St. Paul wrote: "Love is the one thing that cannot hurt your neighbour; that is why it is the answer to every one of the commandments." (Rom 13:10)

Love and forgiveness are your gifts to your ancestors when you pray for healing of your family tree. As your research nears completion, you will begin the process of integration. By sorting and sifting all the data you have gathered, you will prayerfully call upon the Holy Spirit to help you understand who among your ancestors needs forgiveness and why. The many threads of your family story will be woven together into a blanket of love that covers both the living and the dead.

LEMONS OR LEMONADE?

Label this section of your notebook: *Sociological Change*. Outside influences and events have an impact on family life. Some challenges to the family structure include medical advances, wars, terrorist attacks, economic factors, human rights issues, and technological innovations. Rapid changes in technology are responsible for major changes in the way people live, and they fuel the needs and desires of consumers. They also widen the separation between the wealthy and the poor.

1.   How has sociological change benefited or adversely affected generations of your family?

2.   Have you discovered episodes of poverty and its related problems among your ancestors?

3.   Are there heroic stories of how your ancestors coped with economic difficulties?

4.   Did economic misfortune overcome your ancestors and cause them to lose hope? Were there any suicides?

5.   Has anyone in your family history used the stumbling block of poverty as a stepping-stone to achievement and success?

6.   How have traits of courage, despair, failure, or achievement been passed down in your family? Do you see a pattern of such traits?

7.   What serious health problems in your current family can be traced to earlier generations? Is there a pattern?

8.   Does prejudice and intolerance occur within your family? Can you link it to previous generations?

9.   How has war or terrorism impacted your family history? Were there personal losses of life or health due to war or terrorist attacks?

10. How have technological advances affected your family? Better jobs? Loss of jobs? Financial hardship? Monetary gain?

11. Has there been a pattern of educational achievement in your family? Lack of education? Failure at education?

12. In your family, are there patterns of work-related health problems? Disability or inability to work? Genetic diseases? Mental breakdowns?

GUIDE ME ALONG YOUR PATH, LORD

Lord, there are so many complexities in today's world. Though we long for simplicity, we eagerly embrace every new innovation. Help us to see your glory in all creation and to keep our priorities in balance. As I explore my family history, enlighten my mind to understand how the dramatic changes of the 20th century affected my ancestors' lives. Guide me along your path as I gather the many strands of my family's story and bring it to your altar for healing. Amen.

Chapter 7.

1. William Wordsworth, "The Highland Broach," 1831.

2. *Encyclopedia Americana* Vol. 25 (NY: Americana Corporation), 19-24.

3. Emily Croom, *The Genealogist's Companion and Sourcebook* (OH: Betterway Books, 1994), 13.

Rooted in Jesus

8. THE FAMILY CIRCLE

"...if the root is holy, so are the branches."
(Rom 11:16) NAB

We have covered a broad spectrum of family problems that can enlighten your family history research. Your preparation for family healing, however, is not complete without a closer scrutiny of relationships within your immediate family.

Sometimes the nearest problems are the most difficult to see with clarity. Your personal history begins with your parents. It includes their relationship with one another as a married couple, and your relationship with them. Whether you were an only child or a member of a large family also influences your relationships within the family.

WHEN "I DO" BECOMES "I CAN'T"

We are partially shaped by the way we interpret the love our parents share with one another. God fashioned Eve from one of Adam's own ribs, so that she could be Adam's helpmate and companion. (Gn 2:18) Jesus said that a man must leave his parents and cling to his wife, so that the two become as one. He emphasized the permanency of the marital bond by adding, "So then, what God has united, man must not divide." (Mt 19:4-6)

In previous ages, marriage was pre-arranged by parents, often before children reached the age of consent. The married couple might learn to love one another, but love was not the primary consideration. Today, marriage usually occurs between a man and woman who have "fallen in love." True love, in contrast with being "in love," evolves from their survival together through both the good times and the bad. It emerges from the couple's commitment to pull together, to nurture their relationship, and to be one another's best friend.

In a Christian marriage, the bride and groom enter into a covenant, not only with one another, but also with God. By embracing Jesus within the circle of their union, they can count on his sustaining grace to help them work through difficulties and to remain faithful to their vows. Making a marriage succeed, however, is a true labor of love.

Current statistics reveal that nearly half of all marriages end in divorce. In *Why Marriages Succeed or Fail*, University of Washington author John Gottman notes that the hard work of a successful marriage requires patience, compromise, perseverance, and self-sacrifice. A columnist discussing Gottman's book stated that the key to marital success is "not in avoiding conflict altogether, but in learning to resolve conflict effectively." The union that begins with shared hopes and dreams can become fractured if a couple is not realistically prepared for the problems that can arise.[1]

The Marriage Movement is a broad effort by concerned researchers, clergy, family counselors, and others who hope to reverse the divorce trend through pre-marital education, counseling, and other programs.[2] Their goal is to strengthen marriages and to make divorce more difficult.

If you have suffered the trauma of divorce, you already know about the range of emotions and wounding that accompany a divided marriage.

As you prepare your genogram, be alert for patterns of broken marriages in your lineage. Consider the effects of divorce on the parents' offspring. Make note of the ways divorce later influenced the children's adult decisions.

Divorce and remarriage are facts in today's society and some experts predict that stepfamilies will become the predominant family type in the future. Psychologist M. Heller Kalman explains that the majority of families will be built from marital losses, and the mixture of biologically related and non-biologically related family members will add new complexity to family life. "The stage is then set," he says, "for serious conflicts from past relationships to intrude upon the current family life, and legally required financial commitments may well drain the family's resources."[3]

The complexity of relationships between real families and stepfamilies adds to the need for family healing. As you pray about fractures in your family, you can bring these shattered relationships to the Lord. Ask him to break any pattern of divorce inherent in your family tree, and to heal those who have suffered the consequences of broken homes.

BE FRUITFUL AND MULTIPLY

Family is the natural outgrowth of marital love and fidelity. When God blessed Adam and Eve, he told them to be fruitful and multiply. (Gen 1:28) Jesus, because of his divinity, could have chosen any number of ways to redeem the human race. Instead, he freely elected to enter this world as a helpless baby, and to rely upon the love and protection of human parents. Jesus sanctified family and taught us what it means to be family to one another.

When couples cooperate with God in the act of procreation, the conception of a child normally occurs. Without God's involvement, there is no baby. Children are a "sign of God's blessing and of the parents' generosity."[4] Many pregnancies are unplanned and in large families, one more child can represent exhaustion and financial worry for overtired parents. These are aspects to consider in your family history.

When a pregnancy results from an act of violence, the impact on the developing child depends heavily upon the mother's emotional attitude towards the pregnancy. Even though the initial reaction to an unwanted pregnancy may be negative, hearts have been known to change by the time the baby arrives. Infants have a way of charming and bringing forth love from their parents.

It is important to realize that you are a special gift and a sign of God's blessing. This is true even if your birth was unplanned, or if your parents were unmarried at the time of your conception. Regardless of their circumstances, your parents cooperated with God's plan and gave you the gift of life. You are *not* an accident. You have value!

Some pregnancies are the result of a union between two people who either do not want to be parents, or who find themselves unable to accept the responsibility. A woman who carries her baby to full term and places it for adoption expresses a special kind of love for her child. She not only gives the infant life, she sacrifices her own needs so that her child can have the loving home she is unable to provide. If you were raised by adoptive parents, consider yourself twice blessed. A Polish proverb proclaims, "A child is caressed by its mother, but an orphan is caressed by God."

Feelings that your birth mother abandoned you can be brought to Jesus for healing. He knows the love in your mother's heart. He understands her circumstances and the torment she felt in relinquishing her baby. Jesus wants you to experience love and compassion for her situation. Many adoptees have been able to locate their birth parents. If this is important to you, first take the matter to prayer. Sensitivity is essential because some parents feel uneasy about meeting the children they relinquished.[5]

For every unwed mother there is an unwed father. The circumstances that led to their decision not to marry and provide their child with a home may have caused both parents deep pain and sadness. We can't always know why people made the choices they made, but we can pray for reconciliation.

If you gave up your child for adoption, you may feel haunted by remnant feelings of guilt and sadness. Perhaps you can find consolation in a study of 881 adopted adolescents. It found that "the teens reported positive identities, strong family ties and sound psychological health at the same rates as their non-adopted siblings."

In this survey, teens rated themselves as "less withdrawn and less likely to encounter social problems than did their non-adopted peers."[6] If, in spite of this encouraging news, you have a lingering desire to meet your child, you may be able to arrange a reunion.

BUNDLES FROM HEAVEN

The arrival of a baby portends new responsibilities and concerns. Actually, those responsibilities begin long before an infant's birth. When the sperm and ovum join, they form one cell that "contains the complex genetic blueprint for every detail of human development—the child's sex, hair and eye color, height, skin tone." Scientists have documented an amazing story of life in the womb. "The roots of human behavior, develop early—just weeks after conception." Even before a woman knows she is pregnant, the embryo's brain has undergone remarkable formation.[7]

By five weeks, the brain's cerebral cortex, the center of thought, speech, movement, and other abilities, is rapidly developing. At eight weeks, the evolving new life is called a fetus, which means young one or offspring. At nine weeks, the fetus can hiccup and react to loud noises. By the end of the first trimester, the fetus has the ability to feel and to smell, to yawn and to suck. Sonograms often show the fetus sucking its thumb.

At six months, the unborn child experiences the rapid eye movement associated with dreaming, recognizes the mother's voice, and responds to the reading of a familiar story. Activity by the fetus might cause the mother to feel as if she is carrying a gymnasium as her unborn child moves nearly once every minute, performing an amazing stretching and exercise workout. Janet DiPietro, a Johns Hopkins psychologist, has even observed the fetus "walking around the womb by pushing off with its feet."

Another finding reported by Dr. DiPietro is the effect of the mother's stress on her embryo.[8] The child experiences hormonal changes from the mother's system. A pregnant woman may feel happy or sad, healthy or ill, and she may feel loved or unloved. If her emotional state is unstable, the vulnerable child may experience undue stress prior to its birth.

Studies show that the mind records and carefully stores feelings, sensations, and perceptions before birth. Music played for the developing fetus can be recognized by the newborn child. In 1982, I watched my two-month-old grandchild's reaction when she listened to a recording of a mother's heartbeat emanating from within a stuffed bear. She immediately recognized and responded to the familiar soothing rhythmic sound she had heard during her gestation in her mother's womb.

It is possible to grow up with unresolved issues stemming from the time of conception. Sometimes, older children and adults experience mysterious pangs of hurt and loneliness, feelings of worthlessness and abandonment, or of despair and a sense of being unloved. These emotions can arise singly or in combination, with no recognizable connection to the past, and their sudden eruption can be frightening and overwhelming.

Such phantom feelings can have their origin in childhood, but they also may result from the pre-birth experience, when the unborn child shared in its mother's emotional highs and lows. A deep healing of memories removes the pain of such feelings and restores inner wholeness. This aspect of healing is given in-depth coverage in my book, *The Jesus Walk: The Road to Healing Body and Soul.*[9]

AS THE TWIG IS BENT

Children thrive in a home environment that includes involvement with both parents. Ideally, parents help their children to develop self-esteem and to grow towards independence, while providing them with spiritual guidance to help them become strong and morally responsible adults. A healthy home environment requires that adults behave like adults. If the parents haven't resolved their own emotional issues from childhood, they will find it difficult to provide mature direction for their children. John Bradshaw aptly describes this deficiency: "You look like an adult but feel very needy. You feel like the lifeguard on a crowded beach, but you don't know how to swim."[10]

In reality, many parents are ill-prepared for the responsibilities of parenthood. There are no childrearing rules that work for every family in every situation. Your parents probably made some mistakes. Most parents do. Those who received inadequate parenting themselves come to parenthood with their own deep wounding. The Japanese say, "When you have your own children you will understand your obligation to your parents."

As you reflect on your childhood, you may recall times when your needs were unmet or your parents failed to understand you. Sometimes, we get stuck in our childhood emotions of hurt and disappointment. When we continue to dwell on hurt feelings from the past, those memories can prevent us from "growing up" emotionally and becoming whole.

Through the process of family healing, you can experience a new understanding of your parents. By forgiving their mistakes and accepting them just as they are, *and were*, you give them freedom to become all that they are meant to be. Once you unlock your grip on disagreeable memories, or allow those memories to unlock their hold on you, you and your parents can move forward and build a new relationship.

SPECIAL FLOWERS IN THE GARDEN

Children growing up in a large family often envy the attention received by an only child. From my own experience, let me assure you that being the only child is not necessarily a bed of roses. Brothers and sisters have an opportunity for companionship and special bonding with one another, while the only child experiences loneliness and is forced to become self-reliant in many ways. Both situations have pros and cons.

Aside from your parents, perhaps no one knows you better than the brothers and sisters who have seen you at your best and your worst. During your lifetime, your feelings about your siblings might fluctuate between fondness and animosity. It is natural to become frustrated with the people we love. If, however, your problems with your siblings are extreme, reread the section on feuding. Unresolved hostility in a family is destructive.

Grandparents, or aunts and uncles, sometimes step in and fill a void that parents fail to recognize. If this was true in your situation, you can be thankful for that special relationship. Even if your mentor was a godparent or close family friend rather than a blood relative, consider including them on your genogram. Like a tree in the forest that props up a leaning tree, your mentor provided the support you needed. By taking a significant part in your life, this person qualifies as a spiritual relative.

Children who are born with physical or mental limitations require a special kind of love, as do children who suffer from physically limiting diseases. Yet many parents who have cared for children with special needs will tell you that the love returned by these children is extraordinary. In their own way, such children are a special blessing from God.

In years past, generations of a family often lived together or nearby. Today, many families struggle with enormous problems without assistance from relatives. There are 5.75 million Americans who belong to the "caregiver generation." They divide their time between work, raising their children, and caring for aged parents. The emotional stress is compounded when a parent is afflicted with Alzheimer's disease or senile dementia. It is painful to watch a loved one's mental faculties give way to amnesia, confusion, depression, and sometimes, violent behavior.

When life is turned upside down and backwards by illness and catastrophe, the presence of family can be a comfort. Whether you are caring for elderly relatives or raising your grandchildren, you probably feel overburdened, especially if you lack support from family members. Know that God can bring good out of the worst situations by opening avenues of communication and healing old family conflicts.

A HOUSE DIVIDED CANNOT STAND

In every family there are members who do not fit the mold. These are the black sheep, the misfits, the misunderstood, and the difficult to love. Frequently such people are disowned by relatives and are disinherited from family fortunes. Perhaps their names are no longer spoken by family members who feel angry or embarrassed by them. They are like broken, discarded branches on the family tree. Regardless of the ideologies or idiosyncrasies that set outcasts apart in their families, they have a rightful place on the family tree. Wherever they appear in your lineage, there is a double need for healing. The alienated need prayer but so do those who repudiate them.

Serious divisions tear a family apart, causing deep pain. If you cut off your hand, your arm suffers because it can no longer do the things it wants to do. The brain, which continues to receive messages from the nerves, thinks the hand is still there. The arm knows better but is helpless to remedy the situation. Meanwhile, the other arm must do the work of two. The entire body suffers.

With the aid of modern surgery, a severed hand might be restored if it is properly cared for and promptly reattached. In the case of alienated families, however, a great deal of time may have passed since the separation first occurred. Healing is still possible but it requires prayer, forgiveness, patience, and a willingness to reconcile. For healing to occur, hearts must be softened and changed. You can call upon the merciful love of Jesus to heal these family wounds and reunite your family.

Hurt feelings usually underlie anger. Persistent anger frequently spawns irrational beliefs and can lead to long-lasting bitterness. Try to discern the root causes of family separation and brokenness. The character traits involved in estrangement often contribute to other patterns of dysfunction in the family and they will be the focus of your prayers for healing.

Serious rifts develop when material possessions take precedence over relationships. Misunderstandings and disputes over money or assets, a common source of family division, are often documented. Clues to look for in family wills include: terms that favor one or more relative over others, wills that bequeath a token $1.00 to a relative, and outright disinheritance.

In addition to probate records, recorded deeds are a useful source of information about land transfers, deeds of gift, power of attorney, and warranty deeds. Property transfers may have resulted in civil suits, which can be researched in court records. Divorce records also provide considerable information about disputes over property and the custody of children.

Never is the strain of broken family relationships more conspicuous than during holidays and other special family gatherings. In the interest of peace, some members may be invited while others are shunned, leading to increased hurt and alienation within the family network. When you research family photographs, remember that family outcasts may be missing from photos of family reunions. If included, they may appear isolated from the group. You can write a new page in your family's history by encouraging reconciliation.

As forgotten memories rise to the surface, you can expect to shed some tears. Allow yourself to experience the emotions that accompany your tears. Healing is a process and tears help alleviate the pain. The release of tears is a sign that God is already doing a healing work within you. It is confirmation that you are on the right track and a sign that additional healing lies ahead.

UNTANGLING FAMILY ROOTS

Label this section of your notebook: *Family Relations*. By exploring delicate relationships, you prepare for healing.

1. Were you raised by your birth family?

2. What is your adult relationship with your parents?

3. Were you adopted, raised by stepparents or a foster family?

4. Describe your parents' relationship: Loving, nagging, quarrelsome, buddies, trusting, suspicious, ambivalent?

5. Did your parents divorce?

6. Did they remarry?

7. Did their children have to choose between parents?

8. How were their children's lives changed by separation from one parent or the other?

9. How did the parents' divorce affect their children's attitudes towards marriage?

10. As adults, were the children committed to avoiding mistakes their parents made?

11. Or did they repeat the type of behavior that led to their parents broken marriages?

12. Did they resolve not to marry, so as to avoid risking the pain of a broken marriage?

13. How do you feel about divorce today?

14. How can you improve your marriage?

"One climbs up a tree from the root, not from the top."
(Finnish proverb)

Write brief descriptions of your relationships with your husband, parents, brothers, sisters, and grandparents. Include any relationship with a mentor, whether within or outside of the family circle. If you are a parent, describe your relationships with your children and grandchildren.

Think about your important relationships. Suppose you could change them. What would you change? Write down your thoughts.

If you could rewrite your family history, what would change? Spend time imagining the changes. Write a short description of your ideal family, giving relatives the good qualities and traits you feel are missing. As you pray for your family, hold these positive images in your mind.

CREATOR, HEALER, TEACHER

Father God, you created family and you know the strengths and weaknesses within my family. In your divine wisdom, inspire me as I pray for my ancestors and my living family. Help me repair my damaged relationships. Protect all of us from attitudes of judgmentalism. Show us how to have hearts of love and forgiveness. Thank you, Lord, for your faithfulness and your patience as we struggle towards the wholeness you desire for our family. Amen.

Chapter 8.

1.   William R. Mattox, Jr., "Living together fails as trial run," *USA Today*, July 13, 1998, 13A.

2.   Karen S. Peterson, "Making I do Harder to Undo," *USA Today*, July 21, 1998, D1.

3.   M. Heller Kalman, Ph.D., "Family Life," *New England Booming*, May 1998, 25.

4.   *Catechism of the Catholic Church*, 630.

5.   Adoptees and birth parents interested in reuniting can register with the International Soundex Reunion Registry (ISRR), P.O. Box 2312, Carson City, NV 89702. Send a business size, stamped, self-addressed envelope with request for Soundex registration forms.

6. Annie Murphy Paul, "Good news: Adopted kids do just as well." A report on a study conducted by the Search Institute in Minneapolis, MN. *USA Weekend*, January 22-24, 1999), 12-13.

7. "The First Nine Months," Focus on the Family, 1989. Leaflet distributed by Eagle Forum, Alton, IL 62002.

8. Janet L. Hopson, "Fetal Psychology," *Psychology Today*, September/October 1998, 44-48, 76.

9. Patricia A. McLaughlin, *The Jesus Walk: The Road to Healing Body and Soul* (NY/Mahwah, NJ: Paulist Press, 1997), 127-136.

10. John Bradshaw, *Bradshaw On: The Family* (FL: Health Communications, Inc., 1988) 175.

9. EXCAVATING DARK ROOTS

"Let there be light shining out of darkness..." (2 Cor 4:6)

Gardens flourish in the light. Sunshine, good soil, water, and nourishment are all essential to a productive garden. Soil needs cultivation so that it does not become compacted, and weeds must be removed to provide plants the necessary space to flourish. Trees have the same requirements and in spite of their majestic reach toward heaven, they depend upon roots buried deep in the earth. The health of the roots affects the health of the tree, and the same is true with families.

By digging deeper into your family history, you may uncover injured roots that are concealed in pockets of darkness. Dark roots include family secrets, boundary issues, destructive addictions or behaviors, violence, suicide, and contamination of the family lineage by evil.

One of the greatest challenges to family research involves the unearthing of family secrets. The hidden stories families are unwilling to disclose are the very issues that cry out for God's healing touch. Through the disclosure of buried secrets and with prayers for their harmful effects, tremendous family healing can be achieved.

FAMILY SECRETS

Family secrets can involve any aspect of family life that is kept hidden because of real or imagined disgrace. Rather than suffer embarrassment in the community, or perhaps to prevent insinuations of guilt-by-association, some members of a family may conspire to keep silence about family situations that are considered shameful and unspeakable. Such secrets are frequently kept from children in the family, with the noble intention of protecting them. The secrets do not vanish. They merely linger in the shadows.

Family secrets attempt to conceal family behaviors or events that might be considered improper or unacceptable by society. It is not uncommon for families to hide their knowledge of suicides, murder, criminal activity, incest, abuse, abortion, addiction, illegitimacy, mental illness, marital infidelity, scandals, homosexuality, and even illness.

Details of adoption have frequently been shrouded in secret, either to protect the child or the parents. Some government agencies have cooperated in the secrecy by legally sealing birth and adoption documents, to the chagrin of adults seeking their birth parents, as well as to parents seeking reconciliation with the child they relinquished.

Discovering one family secret may lead you on a trail of deeper family dysfunction. According to psychotherapist Cloé Madanes, family secrets about money are frequently linked to sexual secrets, violence, lying, and cheating in other areas. She explains, "Perhaps the reason is that when a basic code of ethics is broken in one area, the whole ethical structure of family life breaks."[1]

At first thought, keeping family secrets might not seem so terrible. The rationale goes something like this: Why should I have to tell anyone else? This is nobody's business but my own (ours)! What will the neighbors (friends, family, fellow-workers) think if they find out? If people hear about this, they won't like me. If this gets out, I might lose my job! If my kids find out about this, they may not love or respect me!

Any or all of the above may be true. What is also true, however, is that family secrets involve a conspiracy to lie. Falsehoods and denial result from a choice to live the fantasy, not the reality. When the truth is shrouded or distorted, the moral fiber of the family is damaged.

Family secrets undermine trust and deprive children of opportunities to think rationally and make good decisions. Psychologist Mary Pipher states, "For families or individuals to be healthy, they must be able to integrate all of their experiences into their lives. Unprocessed experiences block growth and keep people from thinking clearly and realistically."[2] By dealing with reality, we learn resilience, a necessary attribute for coping with and surviving life's difficulties.

Author and therapist John Bradshaw writes and lectures about the fear of disclosure that leads shame-based families to live in denial of their problems. He has aptly defined the toxic shame associated with self-alienation, co-dependency, addiction, and other personality disorders as a type of spiritual bankruptcy.

Bradshaw explains that toxic shame passes down through the generations and is acted out unconsciously. It is characterized by denial, idealization of parents, and repression and dissociation from emotions. Family members are unable to identify the buried roots of shame and pain that underlie these behaviors. "Since it is kept hidden, it cannot be worked out."[3]

Bear in mind that ancestors who kept family secrets probably meant well. Even if their secrecy created problems, their intentions may have been good. It takes considerable skill to know when and how to share private information with children. Your ancestors lived in a different era and may have lacked the education and sophistication which current generations enjoy.

While it is important to be honest, adults who are disclosing sensitive information need to weigh the child's maturity against the level of detail to be shared. It can be harmful to provide more detail than the child can absorb and understand. Information must be shared discretely so that the child can process it in a positive manner. Your intent is to ensure mutual confidence and trust, not to create problems a child cannot handle.

Sometimes, children who ask questions receive answers that are beyond their need to know. You have probably heard the story about Jimmy, who came home from kindergarten and pestered to know where he came from. When the parent finally gave in and explained all the details of sexual reproduction, the boy replied, "Oh, I thought maybe I came from Indiana like my friend Johnny."

Your only purpose in rooting out family secrets should be to bring them out of the dark and into the healing light of Christ. When the roots are healed, health is restored to the family tree.

UNNATURAL TIES THAT BIND

A plant's roots become matted and tangled when they are confined in a container too small to accommodate them. As a result, the rootbound plant is unable to grow and thrive. A similar situation occurs when parents are unwilling to let go of their adult children's lives, or when adults are unable to break free from the perceived constraints of their parents or others.

You can introduce a healthier environment for the rootbound plant by repotting it. My climbing rose bush began with a small cutting that grew to a height of four feet. Although it appeared healthy, it never produced flowers. Then one day, I noticed that the plants leaves had withered and most of the stem had turned brown. The only sign of life was a small strip of green stem emerging from the buried roots.

I trimmed the dead foliage, repotted the plant in a larger container, and within two days new growth appeared! Soon the rose bush could be transplanted outdoors, where it belonged. Then it could become the beautiful flowering plant it was intended to be. Sometimes family relationships need similar care.

Momma, in the cartoon strip by that name,[4] constantly interferes in her grown children's lives. She directs Mary Lou's search for a husband, badgers Thomas about his wife's housekeeping and cooking, and pesters Francis to clean up his room and find a job. Her methods range from nagging to martyrdom to feigning neardeath as she whines, complains, lays guilt on her children, and pines away in loneliness. If confronted, Momma would insist that she loves her kids and only wants what is best for them. Meanwhile, Mary Lou is aggravated and defiant, Thomas and his wife try to please, and Francis manipulates Momma for money. The game is unsatisfying to all, but the players don't know how to break free.

In *Cutting Loose*, Howard M. Halpern shows the transgenerational nature of such child-parent relationships. He describes how the love-starved inner child of the martyred mother learned her behavior from her mother, who learned it from hers. They share a common message, "I'm suffering so you owe me."[5]

The clinging adult child exhibits another type of controlling behavior. Rather than live an autonomous life, this person wants constant reassurance of the parents' love and protection. The parents may feel they have failed, but they frequently exacerbate the problem by leaping at every opportunity to rescue their "helpless child."

There are many variations on this theme. A few examples are: the perpetual college student who relies on parental support *ad infinitum*; the married adult who runs home every time there is a marital conflict; the adult who cannot make a decision without parental approval; and those who try to control relatives through reward and punishment.

As you research your family tree, you will be looking for incidents of bondage. Bondage can take many forms but they all involve control that is out of control. Family members who are deeply enmeshed frequently exhibit controlling behavior, though they may be totally unaware of their strong inclination to control.

Co-dependency has several definitions. Basically, it involves a progressive preoccupation with the needs or actions of others. In this state of emotional dependency, people neglect their own feelings and needs and lose their self-identity. Co-dependency is a downward spiral but it can be reversed and cured.[6]

Unhealthy boundaries occur any time a person misuses others in order to have his or her own needs met. The behavior can be overt, manipulative, or covert. These patterns are often replicated in succeeding generations of a family. One important thing to remember is that it takes two to play the game.

Recognition of the problem is the first step in curing it. While it may be difficult to change one's behavior, change is possible. For the person who finds it difficult to break free of a controlling relationship, therapy can help. The focus must be on self-change. We cannot change others, but we *can* change our own behavior. People in our relationships will often change in response to our new behavior.

Patterns of bondage in your lineage should be noted on your genogram. Your prayers for your family tree may result in the breakthrough that will launch your family into healthier relationships. Freed from emotional bondage, the members can grow strong and forge new and healthy relationships with one another.

THE BONDAGE OF ADDICTION

Many who feel unable to cope with life's stresses and demands turn to alcohol or drugs in order to numb their pain and temporarily hide from unresolved problems. Others may overeat, become work-addicted, or gamble compulsively. Some will starve themselves or turn to self-mutilation. Still others use pornography and become involved in obsessive/compulsive sexual acts.

Any of these actions can lead to addiction as the troubled person finds more and more need for "pain relief." People who suffer from addiction have turned over their freedom to the substances or behaviors that now control their lives. The more they indulge in their addictions, the more pain they feel and the more relief they need. Addiction is a self-defeating loop.

Addictive behavior affects everyone in the family and the tendency is passed on to future generations in one form or another. While there also may be a genetic predisposition to addictive behaviors, there is no simple cure. So much depends upon the addict's motivation to change. The power of God to transform behavior is the most hopeful antidote available. Through our prayers, Jesus can break the trance of addiction in the family and free the addicted to seek help. Healing requires the addicted person's cooperation in the recovery process, through rehabilitation and 12-step programs. Many counseling programs recognize the need to treat the entire family.

SPIRITUAL DECEPTION

Weeds detract from the beauty of the garden and when allowed to flourish, they choke out the healthy plants. According to my gardening book, "If you keep an eye out for small weeds and destroy them when you first see them, your garden should be neat and you'll never have to struggle with large weeds."[7]

This sound advice has practical applications for the spiritual life, as well. The seeds of invasive vegetation quietly open unnoticed and in the early stages of growth, it is difficult to distinguish weeds from flowers. As their roots become entrenched, however, weeds branch out and overpower healthy plants. A wholesome lifestyle is the best insurance against illness, and a healthy spiritual life provides a barrier to spiritual darkness.

Experimentation with the occult is one of the most insidious ways people become bound by forces of darkness. Entrapment can begin with something as simple as reading the daily horoscope for amusement. A person who is unwilling to make a decision without first consulting the horoscope has gone beyond casual interest. When the novelty leads to a habit or an obsession, what began as a lark has evolved into a serious spiritual state called bondage. Bondage is characterized by the erosion of free will. The occult attempts to bind us up. Conversely, Jesus sets us free from sin and darkness.

It has been said that the devil's favorite tool is the simple wedge, and not the sledgehammer as you might suppose. With the wedge, he creates a small opening through which he can slip tendrils of evil. Once it becomes rooted in hidden places, evil is free to flourish like crabgrass and suffocate the spirit.

Our first response is usually, "Oh no! Not me. Not in my family!" Prayerfully examine your family's history to determine if your lineage is free from contamination with evil. The most innocent flirtation with the occult can have profound repercussions.

One way evil may have tainted past generations of Americans, as far back as the 1890s, was through their use of the Ouija board. The game evolved from the French planchette, which during the 1850s gained the attention of Americans who wanted to commune with spirits.[8]

The object of the Ouija, which still enjoys popularity today, is to ask questions and receive "spirit-guided" or telepathic answers. Innocent children, unaware of the dangers of contact with the spirit world, can be easily lured into the occult through this pastime. Other seemingly harmless games, which involve role-playing in a make-believe world of occult intrigue, have been said to cause young people to commit acts of suicide or murder while lost in the fantasy.

Many popular and captivating video and computer games are equally dangerous because of their seductive violence and the acceptance of evil as the norm. The rapidly flickering images in some video games have reportedly caused epilepsy attacks in large numbers of children. With the proliferation of violence on television and in films, there is a corresponding increase of violence among children. Unsupervised access to the Internet further risks a child's exposure to adult-theme chat rooms, pornographic materials, and other harmful media.

As a society, our moral sensitivity has been numbed. The evening news brings murder and police chases right into the living room. Entertainment featuring vulgar language, explicit sex, and outrageous violence is so common it has lost its shock value. A family guided by strong spiritual and moral values is the best insurance against a child's contamination by destructive influences. The choices that a family makes today will impact future generations.

Our current culture of materialism and consumerism can lead to feelings of emptiness and spiritual hunger. As a result, many people are exploring new avenues of spiritual renewal. One byway that attracts seekers is the New Age movement with its emphasis on crystals and channeling of spirits. New Age is really another name for superstition and psychic power, a detour that misleads followers into thinking they will attain spiritual self-fulfillment.

Deceptive practices are always cloaked in terminology that sounds convincing because it contains some element of truth. Just as people are deceived by fortune-tellers who surround themselves with religious images and candles, many are misled by the attractive packaging of New Age practices. They fail to see beyond the veil of deception.

The use of Ouija boards or involvement with tarot cards, astrology, and fortune telling can make one vulnerable to demonic activity. Participation in seances, consultations with curanderos, the reading of tea leaves, and similar practices are dangerous for the same reason.

Evil spawns evil. In *Healing Your Family Tree*, Father John Hampsch, C.M.F. advises that even in the absence of involvement with occult or demonic activities, relatives within the family tree of those who have been involved can be affected. "It is helpful to denounce not only the works of the devil, but also the occult practices of our forefathers, as we submit ourselves to Jesus Christ."[9]

Curses are a source of evil that can afflict a family without their knowledge or involvement. The effects, depending on the nature of the curse, can include problems such as illness, financial losses, violent deaths, and suicides. Did any of your ancestors have enemies who might have wished them serious harm?

Involvement of your ancestor in the practice of satanism, with its blatant worship of evil, might lead you to suspect a family curse. In addition, many ancient cults worshipped pagan deities. Practices of superstition, divination, and black magic in conjunction with spirit worship still prevail in some parts of the world. Have any of your relatives been involved in such practices? If so, they are in special need of your prayers. While you may not like the sin, you can feel compassion and love for the sinner.

Passivity is another spiritual danger. We cooperate with evil when we refuse to take it seriously. If we dismiss the evil one as myth, we have already welcomed his entry by dropping our guard. Jesus taught us to take a stand against evil. During his ministry, he delivered many from demonic control and he taught us to pray, "...lead us not into temptation but deliver us from evil."

If you suspect that your lineage has been contaminated by curses from any source, begin praying at once. Call upon the power of Jesus to set your family free. Ask him to surround you and your family with his holy angels for protection. Pray this prayer often.

Evil has no power over you when you stay close to Jesus. If you have been involved in the occult, make a firm resolution to avoid such activities in the future. Cleanse your house of any books, charms, or other objects that symbolize your interest in or your allegiance to evil. Objects which represent evil are powerless unless we give them power. Our attachment to them, however, indicates our unwillingness to let go of our evil inclinations.

THE LIGHT OF THE WORLD

Jesus is the Light of the world. (Jn 8:12) He wants to free your family from the chains of darkness. Falsehoods distort and disguise facts, creating doubt and confusion. Bondage (to people, substances, or forces of evil) shackles us, enslaves us, and keeps us in the dark. Truth is the key that opens doors. When the light of Christ enters, there can be no darkness, no doubt, no confusion.

Jesus defeated evil by his suffering and death on the cross. His victory is ours to share. By his stripes, by his wounds, by his precious blood, we are saved. As children of the Father and heirs to heaven, we have the right to claim the power of Jesus' precious blood to free ourselves and our families from demonic influences. When we call upon the name of Jesus, he cleanses our bloodlines and protects us under his mantle of love.

ROOTS THAT CLUTCH

Label this section of your notebook: ***DARK SHADOWS***.

1.   Have you identified your family's black sheep, the outcasts, the alienated, the unloved?

List them.

2.   What divisive factors have caused pain in your family? (money, property, divorce, custody battles, etc.)

3.   Family secrets hide shame-based "unspeakable acts" which threaten to jeopardize livelihood, reputation in the community, or love and respect in the family. What family secrets have you uncovered?

4.   In what ways do your family members attempt to control one another? Can you identify a generational pattern?

5.   What addictions, if any, occur in your family?

6.   Have family members participated in occult activities or pagan worship?

7.   Do you know of any evil curses pronounced against a member or a branch of your family?

8.   How many words can you form from the word evil? Which one do you choose? (answers at bottom of page)

9.   Read the following Scriptures: Rom 8:38; Eph 6:12.

10. Have you prayed to Jesus for your family's deliverance from evil, and for his protection? If not, why are you waiting? What holds you back?

Answers: lie vie vile veil live

Meditate on the words of Jesus:
> I am the way and the truth and the life. No one comes to the Father except through me. (Jn 14:6)

Meditate on the promise of Jesus:
> If you remain in my word...you will know the truth, and the truth will set you free. (Jn 8:32-33)

HEALING DARK ROOTS

Lord Jesus, I offer you my broken family and I implore you to bless and heal our dark roots. Set us free from any addictions that have passed down through family generations. On behalf of all generations of my family, I apologize for any involvement in the occult, whether past or present. I beg forgiveness for the times we have been guilty of disloyalty to you. Cleanse my family of all contamination with evil, Lord Jesus. Sever our connections with any and all objects, activities, or groups that might lure us away from you.

Grant us your divine protection on our lives, Jesus. Help me to forgive my ancestors for any actions or curses that have caused misfortune for my family. Give us the strong resolve to keep our eyes focused on your light, your truth, and your way. All this I pray in your holy name, Jesus. Amen.

Chapter 9.

1. Cloé Madanes with Claudio Madanes, *The Secret Meaning of Money: How It Binds Together Families in Love, Envy, Compassion or Anger* (SF, CA; Jossey-Bass Inc., 1994), 32-33.

2. Mary Pipher, Ph.D., *The Shelter of Each Other: Rebuilding Our Families* (NY: G.P. Putnams Sons, 1996), 143.

3. John Bradshaw, *Bradshaw On: Healing the Shame That Binds You* (FL: Health Communications Inc., 1988), Chapter 1; 32.

4. Mell Lazarus, *Momma* (Creators Syndicate, Inc.).

5. Howard M. Halpern, Ph.D., *Cutting Loose: An Adult Guide to Coming to Terms With Your Parents* (Toronto, NY: Bantam Books/ Simon and Schuster, 1976), 36-37.

6. *Healing the Child Within*, 28-29.

7. *Sunset New Western Garden Book* (CA; Lane Publishing Co. 1967), 67.

8. Colin McEnroe, "In Touch With the Beyond — Or Is It Balderdash?" *Los Angeles Times*, November 26, 1992, W3.

9. John H. Hampsch, C.M.F., *Healing Your Family Tree* (Santa Barbara, CA: Queenship Publishing Co., 1997), 126-127.

Rooted in Jesus

10. GOING HOME

"I am going now to prepare a place for you." (Jn 14:2)

Death is "the homecoming for which the soul was created."[1] Christians believe that death is a transformation, not an ending. The body is mortal and finite; however, the soul, which gives it life, does not perish when the body dies.

The Church teaches that the soul is meant to return to the Creator, either immediately upon death or after a period of purification. Hell, a place of total separation from God's presence, is reserved for those who die unrepentant in a state of grave sin. At the final Resurrection, the soul will be reunited with the body.[2] I believe that our compassionate and merciful God so loves all of his children, he gives each one unlimited opportunities to choose eternal life with him, even during the final gasps of life.

Love and concern among family members goes beyond the grave. It is through the love of Christ that your prayers for family healing span the separation between the living and the dead. We became members of the Body of Christ through baptism. Therefore, it is through him that our families are connected both in life and in death.

By his death and resurrection, Jesus won our victory over death and claimed our souls for eternal glory with him and the Father. We know that our eternal reward far outshines anything the world can offer. Yet, in spite of this promised salvation, we struggle against the thought of leaving the life we know on earth.

In your pursuit of healing for your family tree, you must confront death, which is a certainty for everyone. It is important to discover, not only how your ancestors lived, but how they died. You also need to determine if any family members still grieve for deceased relatives, and what unfinished business your ancestors left as part of their legacy. In addition, knowing about their illnesses will help you discern the need for prayer about generational patterns of disease.

THE SEEDS OF WELLNESS

For the majority of humans, death is one event we are neither ready for, nor anxious to experience. Experts who study and compile longevity data give credit to factors such as luck, personality, social and economic conditions, genetics, and lifestyle. Luck is happenstance. Considerable effort is required to change one's personality, but personal growth is achievable. A positive attitude and determination have helped many to rise above socioeconomic conditions and misfortune. It is within our power to change our lifestyles but genetics are beyond our control.

Health researchers are discovering significant links between genetics and genealogy. It is known that specific racial or ethnic groups are more vulnerable to certain diseases. Cystic fibrosis is more common to Caucasians of Northern & Western European ancestry. Tay-Sachs, a recessive disorder, often afflicts infants of Central and Eastern European Jewish descent. The major diseases that affect Americans and tend to "run in families" are heart disease, diabetes, and some forms of cancer.[3] Sickle cell anemia occurs primarily in people of African descent, though it can occur in people from Italy, Greece, Arabia, and India.[4]

The Human Genome Project, an effort to decode the entire sequence of genetic instructions for the human body, will hopefully lead to the cure or prevention of many illnesses. This is encouraging for the offspring of 20 million Americans who are carriers of true genetic defects. It is actually feasible that one day we will be able to grow new body parts to replace aging or diseased organs and limbs. In the meantime, we must all confront the reality of sickness and eventual death.

Most people yearn to live a long life, free of serious illness. As Stanford neuroscientist Robert Sapolsky points out, there are other factors to consider in illness besides genetics, because nature and nurture interact. "A gene, a stretch of DNA, does not produce a behavior. A gene does not produce an emotion, or even a fleeting thought. It produces a protein."[5] Those proteins include the system of hormones and the way they function in our response to stimuli. Genes can affect *how* we respond to our environment, but they don't tell the whole story.

The seeds of wellness are sown in the family, where lifestyle has its beginnings. There is a mind-body-spirit factor which influences health for better or for worse. It is possible to change unhealthy attitudes and behavior, and the good habits that promote wellness can be learned.

Since heart disease and cancer have identifiable links to lifestyle as well as to genetics, there are positive steps a person can take for improved health. A balanced diet, moderate exercise, avoidance of harmful substances, and careful attention to stress management help improve one's prospects for longevity. These are steps that can only be taken by the individual. No one else can do it, not even God.

Your prayers about the attitudes and behaviors handed down from past generations invite the grace of God to counterbalance inherited ancestral defects in your family and to inspire motivation, where needed, to correct poor health habits.

FLIRTING WITH DEATH

Youth, a formative stage which should reflect glowing health and vitality, has become an age group sadly characterized by risky behaviors that all too often end in early death. A report from the National Center for Health Statistics on the deaths of 37,000 young people every year shows that 62% of the deaths in ages 5-24 are preventable.

The Center reports that deaths of young people from homicide (18%) and suicide (12%) exceed those caused by injuries (11%), while HIV infection accounts for 2%. Nearly 10,000 deaths (27%) are due to diseases, including: cancer, birth defects, heart disease, stroke, pulmonary disease, flu, and influenza. An overwhelming number of young people (30%) die in motor vehicle accidents, half of which are linked to alcohol.

Patterns of drinking, smoking, drug use, sexual promiscuity, and violent behavior contribute to the early deaths of young males, while girls are more prone to having distorted body image and suicidal ideations.[6] Even though a shocking number of young people are taking prescribed medication for depression, the suicide rate among teens and young adults remains alarmingly high.

Teen behaviors of smoking, unhealthy diet, and lack of exercise usually continue into adulthood, placing them at greater risk for heart trouble and cancer. The mental attitudes that predispose young people to destructive behavior may also affect their emotional and physical well-being later in life.

Researchers studying the psychological elements of sickness believe that people who react pessimistically to life's difficulties in youth are more likely to encounter poor health by early midlife. Accidents can happen to people at any age but a reckless flirtation with disaster increases one's susceptibility to accidents. The person who takes unrealistic risks may be saying that life is not worth living.

Do you have a family member who lives constantly on the edge, like an accident waiting to happen? Are there signs of depression among the young people in your family? Pray for discernment so that you can better understand their needs. What deep despair prevents them from wanting to live a long and productive life? You can pray for a release from harmful attitudes and behaviors that threaten your offspring's health and mortality.

Youth violence has become a national concern as increasing numbers of teens and pre-teens vent their anger through acts of assault and murder. Prompt recognition of problems and early intervention can help prevent tragic violent outbursts by young people. The National School Safety Center offers a helpful checklist for evaluating a juvenile's risk factor for committing violence.[7]

As we learn more about the causes of violent behavior, we may be able to prevent it in the future. *Ghosts from the Nursery* cites the harmful effects of neglect and child abuse in the first years of life as a contributing factor in the eruption of violent behavior later. The authors state, "Prenatal development and the first two years are the time when the genetic, organic and neurochemical foundations for impulse control are being created."[8]

Is there a history of violence in your family? If so, you should consider the possibility of inherited traits that may have links to violent behavior. Look for ancestral patterns of traumatic or violent deaths, criminal behavior, and issues of abuse within the family. "The apple doesn't fall far from the tree." (Yiddish proverb)

FORMED IN THE WOMB

When God empowered Jeremiah to be his prophet, he said, "Before I formed you in the womb I knew you; before you came to birth I consecrated you." (Jer 1:4-5) We have God's own word that from the very beginning the human embryo is a viable person consecrated by him. Your parents' 23 chromosomes and approximately 50,000 genes combined at the moment of conception to create your physical attributes. Your intelligence and personality were encoded and the essence of who you are was already established.[9]

Early termination of a life in the womb produces parental anguish, whether it results from a miscarriage, a stillbirth, or an abortion. The natural, spontaneous termination of a pregnancy before the twentieth week of gestation is called a miscarriage; after that time, it is a stillbirth. Abortion is an unnatural intervention that causes the unborn child's death and expulsion from the mother's womb. All of these situations cause grief and indicate a deep need for healing.

Healing the Greatest Hurt[10] describes some of the ways that unresolved grief over the loss of an unborn infant affects a woman's life. The authors also describe remarkable family healings that occurred when parents were able to complete their grief for unborn babies and release them to the loving care of Jesus.

The covert act of abortion is an uncreative, violent solution to the natural and creative act of procreation. Standard medical practice requires informed consent from patients or their legal guardians prior to surgery and inherently risky or invasive procedures. Ironically, no one represents the legal rights of the unborn child prior to the abortion that will end its life.

You may have seen films or read about the horrifying details of an abortion procedure. Some explicit materials incite anger and encourage people to take militant action against abortionists. Meanwhile, the verbal rhetoric between pro-life and pro-choice continues. What is frequently obscured, however, is the deep need for healing of those involved in an abortion. Since the abortion of a baby is frequently kept secret, the light of Christ is needed to touch and heal that which is hidden in the dark.

Abortion is traumatic for the baby, but it also leaves scars on the entire family. This violent act is so contrary to the natural inclinations of a woman to nurture and preserve her child's life, we find it difficult to understand the desperation and panic that cause a mother to resort to abortion. While the abortion pill (RU-486) simplifies the terminal procedure, it is unlikely to eliminate the feelings of remorse and shame that accompany the destruction of one's unborn child.

The symptoms of post-abortion syndrome are similar to those of post-traumatic stress disorder. They might include "insomnia or repeated nightmares, loss of appetite, extreme sensitivity, unexplained crying, body tremor, hand wringing, and attacks of uncontrollable anxiety."[11] Doctor McAll's list, based on records of nearly three thousand patients studied during a decade, includes physical and spiritual symptoms as well as numerous emotional difficulties. Problems related to unmourned abortions were not limited to the person undergoing the abortion. Other family members suffered serious problems as well.

Fathers of the unborn often need healing, whether they encouraged the abortion, remained passive about it, or because their protests against it were ignored. Dr. Kenneth McAll describes the deeply hidden emotional wounds of children who survive an attempted abortion. He also documents cases in which children suffered greatly because of their sibling's abortion.[12] In his experience, there is a very high cure rate when such unresolved grief is brought to the Lord for healing.

For a woman who has aborted her baby, overpowering feelings of guilt often surface in midlife, after years of denial. Trained and compassionate volunteers are available to offer confidential and non-judgmental companionship on the healing journey through Project Rachel.[13] In an atmosphere of confidentiality, this outreach provides reconciliation and healing for those suffering from post-abortion syndrome.

If you know or even suspect that someone in your family had

an abortion, ask Jesus to help you regard that person with compassion. It is not your place to judge anyone. Regardless of the events that led your ancestor or family member to such a drastic action, God's mercy and forgiveness are unlimited. Through your prayers for your family tree, you can bring your family's anguish over the loss of unborn babies to the altar of the Lord for healing.

THE GOLDEN AGE

Many family issues that require prayer are focused on the younger generation, but those in the older generation have their share of problems too. Some afflictions of old age are unavoidable but those caused by negligence and poor health habits are preventable. Careless lifestyle, poor self-image, negative attitudes, and depression, are problems for the aged as well as for the young.

Midlife is a time of reflection that offers people the option to change, to be transformed. Those unwilling to risk change and resolve their life problems miss the opportunity to achieve a happier, more fulfilling life. Age brings its own special blessings, including the wisdom acquired in life, and a more relaxed lifestyle, with leisure time for hobbies, volunteer work, and further development of talents.

How well a person adapts to old age depends a lot on mental attitude. Those who grow old without experiencing healing of old inner hurts may view the golden years with anger and bitterness. Some withdraw socially and spend their final years in lonely isolation, while their ability to care for themselves deteriorates. Some elders cling stubbornly to their independence, denying any need for help.

The difficulties of the elderly greatly impact the lives of their adult children, who often serve as their caretakers. Your discussion of the past with your elderly relatives may help relieve some of the tension that exists between the generations. You may find yourself challenged to find a creative balance between sensitivity and tough love. You needn't face these difficulties alone. Invite Jesus into your relationships and invoke the discernment of the Holy Spirit when you are faced with difficult decisions regarding your elderly parents.

SAYING GOODBYE

Death is rarely neat and tidy. If it happens suddenly and without warning, we feel cheated. We may even feel angry. Sudden death robs us of the opportunity to prepare. There are last words we needed to say. We are denied closure, the opportunity to say goodbye. Often there are pangs of guilt. Why didn't I do more when I had the chance? Why didn't I express my love and gratitude before it was too late?

On the other hand, a lingering death demands patience from both the patient and the caregivers. It places a tremendous strain on the entire family. No matter how much you love your lingering relative, it is not uncommon to experience extreme fatigue. Feelings of frustration, helplessness, and martyrdom may arise. "I'm so tired! I give and give of myself but there seems to be no end to it." "No matter how much I do, it's never enough. It isn't fair!" Neither situation is easy.

"Death's an old joke, but it comes fresh to everyone," said Bazarov, in *Fathers and Sons*.[14] No matter how well prepared we think we are for the death of a loved one, especially one who is advanced in age or critically ill, death always catches us by surprise.

It was an ordinary Monday. After a full day of shopping and running errands, I had considered stopping by to visit my parents. Instead, I hurried home to prepare for my weekly prayer meeting.

The phone was ringing when I arrived at my house. My husband was calling to tell me that my father was in the emergency room. He told me Daddy was too tired to talk and needed rest. I could visit him at the hospital the next morning. He said that since prayers were what my father needed most, I should go to the prayer meeting and pray. Reluctantly, I followed my husband's advice.

Just three days earlier, my eighty-six-year-old father had appeared well. In fact, he had been pedaling on his exercise bike. When he became ill over the weekend, my mother grew concerned but Daddy did not want to see a doctor. It was only when his situation became critical that Mother tried to reach me, probably around the same time that I decided not to stop by their apartment for a visit. This is the type of situation that later plagues us with the question, "If only I had...."

When I returned home from the prayer meeting that evening, the phone was ringing again. This time, a doctor informed me that my mother had been unable to make an important decision and since he was unable to reach me, he had placed Daddy on a ventilator. This was far more serious than I had realized.

It was close to midnight when we arrived at my father's bedside in Intensive Care. When I saw his precarious condition, I called for a priest. Daddy's eyes were unfocused and he thrashed about as he received the Sacrament of the Sick. He was trying to recognize the unfamiliar voice at his bedside that said, "Tom, I hope you make it but if you don't, you'll go straight to heaven. All your sins are forgiven."

Moments later, my father slipped into a deep coma. There was only time for me to say, "I love you, Daddy." Within a few hours his kidneys failed and there was irreversible brain damage. By morning he was gone, the victim of pneumonia and an unidentified septic infection.

REST IN PEACE

There are no shortcuts through the grief process. It has to be worked through in stages, and while caring people can provide love and support, no one can do it for you.

For six years following my father's death, my mother suffered terribly from depression and grief. She may have felt remorse because she had not yet taken him for his flu shot, even though he did have the flu. Rather than discuss her feelings, she lashed out at the hospital staff for allowing her husband to die. She also lashed out at me. I can imagine her tormented thoughts: "How much different things might have been, if only...."

Meanwhile, her health declined and she finally agreed to move to a facility that would provide her with 24-hour assistance. She made numerous trips to the emergency room and I learned to be ready, on a moment's notice, to jump in the car and spend long hours there with her.

During that time, I attended a weekend conference on healing the family tree. At the first night's Liturgy, Jesus showed me that Mother was still clinging to Daddy. In my mind, I saw her clenched fists trying to pull him back to earth. Since she was unable to let go of him, I prayed on her behalf for Daddy's release into the full presence of the Lord. I also asked Jesus to fill my mother with his peace.

On my way home Sunday, I visited her and brought her Eucharist. Mother *was* peaceful! Before leaving her room that evening, I noticed that only a drop of water remained in the little holy water font near her bed. I used it to bless her forehead with the sign of the cross. She, in turn, reached up from her bed and blessed me. For me, that was a profound moment of healing in our relationship.

When I brought her Eucharist again the following Saturday, I was stunned by what she told me. "Your father has been here with me all week," Mother said. "It was so nice to have him here." Startled, I asked her how he looked. "Oh, he looked wonderful!" she said. "He looked so happy!" She couldn't remember if he had spoken to her but she had simply enjoyed his presence.

My mother's mind was still sharp and clear, even at the age of eighty-eight. There is no logical explanation for her experience, but I believe God permitted her to have a vision of my father. He answered my prayers for her peace by showing her that Daddy was happy, and that death was not something to be feared. I realized then that God was preparing Mother for death. He was going to call her home.

Five days later, my mother was admitted to the hospital for the last time. She was not dying of bladder cancer, as we had expected she would. Nor was her heart failing, though she had been treated previously for congestive heart failure. She wasn't there for her emphysema, her high blood pressure, or a stroke, even though she had suffered many mini-strokes.

Because of her fragile health, surgery was out of the question for Mother's intestinal blockage. Her doctor asked me to make the decision to let her die and he promised they would keep her comfortable. Nothing in life had prepared me to make such a tough decision. Mother had lived with so much denial, always terrified of death and refusing to talk about it. Now I had to choose for her.

I am a survivor. For myself, I always choose life and trust in Jesus. The decision to do nothing went against everything I believe in, but the doctors insisted that surgery would neither improve her condition nor would it extend her life.

I gave in and called for the priest to anoint Mother. The next day, a friend who is a priest prayed over her and told her, as I had, that Jesus and my father were waiting for her to join them. It was all right for her to go. He fully expected her to sink into a deep coma. She didn't.

The most difficult part was watching Mother suffer. Her pain was excruciating and I spent every day at her bedside, insuring that she was medicated and comfortable.Mother remained semi-comatose except for brief moments when family members came to say goodbye. As he prayed at her bedside, her youngest grandchild asked, "Grandma, do you pray?" "Of course," she answered. "Do you know Jesus loves you?" he asked. She replied emphatically, "Jesus loves everyone!"

From time to time, a nurse would enter the room and say, "Hello, Ruth! How are you?" Mother's eyes would pop open and she would answer brightly, "I'm fine." Then she would slump back into her comatose state. Finally she was given a morphine drip to control her pain. Through it all, she never spoke to me, though she became agitated whenever I left the room. All she wanted was for me to be there. I thought about the many hours we had spent together at her doctors' appointments, on shopping trips, and having lunch. She had always ended our visits by saying, "We never have time to talk." Exasperated, I would reply, "Mother, we have been together all day. What do you want to talk about?" I never found out.

Nurses told me that hearing is the last sense people lose. Even in a coma they can hear. One day I held Mother's hand and leaned close. "Mother, I love you. If you can hear me, squeeze my hand." She did. I told her the things I needed to say, apologized for the times I hurt her, and forgave her for the times she had hurt me. I needed reconciliation and closure, and it was comforting to know that she heard me.

As the morphine overpowered her pain, Mother's slumber grew deeper but her condition seesawed. One day her kidneys were failing. The next day they functioned. One day her heart weakened. The next day it grew strong. At times it seemed that she might recover. The doctors were baffled. They had expected her to die within two days. Her ordeal lasted ten days.

Finally, I realized she was rebelling. We had told her she could leave us, but my mother was a strong-willed, independent woman. I leaned close to her ear and said, "Mother, whatever you do is up to you. You can stay or you can go. I will help you any way I can, whatever you decide to do."

That day I watched my mother's countenance change. By evening, her face was young and beautiful again. Not a wrinkle or a frown. Previously, her forehead had been ridged with pain. I could feel peace in the room and I was certain God had sent the angels I had requested to surround her. The moment of death seemed near and I waited late.

More than twenty-four hours passed before Mother slipped her earthly bonds and fell into the embrace of Jesus. She died as she had lived, with determination and conviction. She did it her way, on her terms. She had to be in control of her death, just as she had fought for control in life.

Her funeral was on St. Patrick's Day and her body was cremated on the feast of St. Joseph. I recalled how much she had loved birds and how she had enjoyed seeing the swallows return to Capistrano Mission on St. Joseph's Day. Mother's remains were buried in my father's grave, at noon on Good Friday. It was a sunny and pleasant day, but at 3 p.m. a storm broke. Even in her death, Jesus was speaking to me. He is so generous with his love and consolation.

My mother lived two years longer than her doctors predicted, and even in dying she greatly surpassed their expectations. People have been known to postpone their death until a meaningful event has passed or some unfinished business is completed. The will to live is more powerful than we realize.

How did your loved ones die? Did they pass peacefully or did they leave kicking and screaming? How did you accept their deaths? Was there time for you to say goodbye? Did you apologize or accept their forgiveness for any slights or misunderstandings? What unfinished business still requires your attention and prayers?

GRIEF AND RELEASE

Nothing prepares us for the loss of our parents. I thought I was prepared during the last two years of my mother's life because her health was so fragile. In the weeks following her death, however, time and again I caught myself thinking I should pick up a carton of ice cream and take it to Mother. I was so accustomed to shopping for the little things that pleased her, I often forgot she was no longer alive.

The goodness of a loving God, the comfort of knowing she is at peace, and the joy of knowing she rests in Jesus' arms with no more pain and misery—all of those facts helped me to feel happy for her. Still, I felt a deep loss. I had become an orphan. It took time to recover.

Grief is a process that cannot be rushed. It comes with strong emotions, feelings of pain and sadness. A person might feel anger towards the person who died and abandoned him. Many experience guilt because of what they did or didn't do for the deceased. Fear and anxiety about the future can paralyze a person who is unaccustomed to making decisions. These emotions follow no set order and they can reappear. It is important to know that grief is not permanent. Recovery is possible.

A grief support group brings together people who share about their losses and help one another to work through the sorrow and heartache. When grief is protracted over a long period of time, counseling can help bring about closure. If the bereaved person suffers a prolonged loss of appetite and expresses an unwillingness to go on living, professional intervention is indicated.

If you have lost someone without the opportunity to express your love, or before you could mend your relationship, it is not too late. You can ask Jesus to be the courier of your love and apologies. Since God exists in eternity, his healing is not limited by time. He is the "I Am"—always present.

One day we will all be whole, body and spirit, in the final resurrection. There will be no sickness, no pain, and no death. Blind eyes will see. Ears will hear clearly. Severed limbs will be restored. Families will be reunited.

> For us, our homeland is in heaven, and from heaven comes the saviour we are waiting for, the Lord Jesus Christ, and he will transfigure these wretched bodies of ours into copies of his glorious body. (Ph 3:20-21)

HOLY LIGHT AT THE END OF THE TUNNEL

Label this section of your notebook: *DECEASED RELATIVES*.

When Lazarus emerged from the tomb, his hands and feet were bound and a burial cloth still covered his face. Jesus told his family, "Unbind him, let him go free." (Jn 11:43)

1. Who among your deceased family members do you miss the most?

2. Is there something you needed to say?

3. Are there unnatural attachments to deceased relatives in your family?

4. Have there been experiences of earth-bound spirits?[15]

5. Are there any babies who were unnamed or not given a Christian burial?

6. Does any family member suffer from the trauma of lost or aborted babies?

7. Were there deaths from accidents, suicide, violence?

8. Were there any unmourned deaths in your family?

Scripture forbids us to communicate with the dead through trances, seances, and other means. Sometimes, however, those who are dead seem to penetrate unseen boundaries and communicate with the living. A woman beset with grief over the sudden death of her father was comforted by his voice telling her not to be sad because he was in a wonderful place. This helped her accept his death.

My mother's sister told about a dream she experienced just five days before her ninety-second birthday: There was a family reunion. Everyone in the family was there, including those who had died. In the next scene, my aunt was in bed asleep and my mother suddenly began shaking her shoulder to awaken her.

My aunt reported that this dream, which occurred almost a year after her sister's death, had seemed very real. Nearly two years later, my aunt died suddenly and unexpectedly from an advanced cancer that may been developing at the time of her dream.

Is it possible that my mother was trying to warn her sister about the impending cancer? We may never know.

You may have heard similar stories from family and friends. Are these coincidences? Fancies of the imagination? Such messages usually have a numinous quality that sets them apart from ordinary dreams or experiences. They appear holy and spiritual in nature, as opposed to ghostly apparitions of troubled spirits. In his mercy, perhaps God chooses to comfort us, to ease our grief over the loss of a loved one. I know of no other way to explain the messages that people receive from the dead in visions and dreams.

SPEAK LORD, YOUR SERVANT LISTENS

Lord, the beautiful mystery of life is outdone by the overwhelming mystery of death. We cling to life and relationships, and struggle to remain here in the life we know on earth. Help us to release our departed loved ones to your care. Fill us with the peace of knowing that life in your divine presence is better than anything this temporal life can offer. Prepare us for the day when we too shall glory in your eternal presence. Amen.

Chapter 10.

1. *The Jesus Walk: The Road to Healing Body and Soul*, 152.

2. *Catechism of the Catholic Church*, 292, 289.

3. Myra Vanderpool Gormley, "Coming to Grips With Heredity," *LA Times Magazine*, part 2, April 29, 1990.

4. *The American Medical Association Family Medical Guide*, ed. Jeffrey R. M. Kunz, M.D. and Asher J. Finkel, M.D. (NY: Random House, 1987), 429.

5. Robert Sapolsky, "A Gene for Nothing," *Discover*, October 1997), 40-46.

6. Steve Sternberg, "Teen-agers in turmoil," *USA Today*, October 5, 1998), D1.

7. National School Safety Center, 4165 E. Thousand Oaks #290, Thousand Oaks, CA 91362-3815, (805) 373-9977.

8. Review by Mary Jo Kochakian, "What happens in infancy may cause violence later," *The Hartford Courant*. In The *Burlington Free Press*, January 17, 1998, 3D.

9. "What They Never Told You About the Facts of Life." Pamphlet distributed by the Human Development Resource Council, Inc., 3941 Holcomb Bridge Road, Norcross, Georgia 30092-2292, (770) 447-1598.

10. Matthew Linn, Dennis Linn, Sheila Fabricant, *Healing the Greatest Hurt* (Ny/Mahwah, NJ: Paulist Press, 1985), Chap. 7.

11. Dennis Coon, *Introduction to Psychology: Exploration and Application* (MN: West Publishing, 1986), 492-493.

12. Dr. Kenneth McAll, *A Guide to Healing the Family Tree* (CA: Queenship Publishing Co., 1996), 107-122.

13. Project Rachel; 1-800-5WE-CARE for confidential referrals in your area. (*www.marquette.edu/rachel*)

14. Ivan Turgenev, *Fathers and Sons*, 1861; trans. Constance Garnett. *The Continental Edition of World Masterpieces* Vol.2, ed. Maynard Mack (NY: W.W. Norton & Co. Inc., 1956), 744.

15. Kenneth McAll writes of earth-bound spirits whose presence is manifested as ghosts. (*see* Books). John Hampsch, C.M.F., explains this phenomenon in *Healing Your Family Tree*.

Rooted in Jesus

11. THE DISCERNMENT PROCESS

*"To remember the past is to commit
yourself to the future."* (John Paul II)

Remembering the past is an important aspect of generational healing, but memory is only the first step in the discernment process. Learning how to understand and utilize those memories for family healing demands perseverance.

According to memory expert Daniel L. Schacter, the memories that help us reconstruct the past are dispersed in various locations of the brain's cortex. In order to use them, we must retrieve and assemble the scattered pieces. While your memory of a situation may not be entirely accurate, the emotions that accompany the memory are probably reliable. Schacter states, "Our recollections of the general contours of our lives—how happy we were as children, the characteristics of parents, siblings, classmates and friends, while not entirely free of subjective biases, are basically accurate."[1]

It is exciting when the answers you seek finally break through, but the moment of "aha!" may first require a lot of inner work. Memory, dreams, intuition, stories, the comments of another, and new information—all can assist your discernment. Meanwhile, continue to pray and trust in the inspiration of the Holy Spirit to bolster your intuition.

One way the Holy Spirit can enlighten you is through your reading and meditation on the inspired words of Holy Scripture. Supplement your evaluation of data by allowing God's words in Scripture to speak directly to your heart. Learning about the life and struggles of biblical characters may help bring to mind similar virtues or defects in your ancestors.

ANCIENT STORIES

Isaac, who had been richly blessed by Yahweh, was a victim of family deception in his own house. Jacob, with help from his conniving mother, deceived his father Isaac. As a result, Esau was cheated out of his rightful blessing as the firstborn son. Later, Jacob himself was deceived. After working seven years so that he could marry Laban's daughter Rachel, he was tricked into marrying her sister Leah instead. Ultimately, he married both women but Rachel remained barren and the family's legacy of deception continued down the lineage. Perhaps similar patterns of deception have occurred through generations of your family.

The story of Joseph, who was sold into slavery by his jealous brothers, is a tale of fatherly love and favoritism, sibling rivalry, jealousy, deception, and mourning. On his deathbed, the aged Jacob blessed his sons, saying, "Joseph is a fruitful creeper near the spring, whose tendrils climb over the wall." (Gn 49:22)

Joseph, who had risen above his circumstances, told the brothers who had wronged him that it was not his place to judge them. In a dramatic episode that ends with reconciliation and family healing, he not only forgave them, he promised to take care of them and their families. This story provides a powerful model for the reconciliation of family disagreements and hurts. (Gn 27-50)

Scripture is filled with stories of heroism, weakness, bravery, and cowardice. Moses was abandoned by his mother at the age of three months. Yet her act of courage saved her son from death because Pharoah had decreed that all newborn Hebrew boys were to be drowned in the river. When Moses was found among the reeds by Pharoah's daughter, the infant's own sister came forward and offered to find a Hebrew woman (her mother) to nurse him. After living with his true mother and family for three years, he was adopted by Pharoah's daughter and was raised as an Egyptian prince. The orphan Moses was later directed by God to lead the Israelites out of bondage in Egypt. (Book of Exodus)

Moses appears to have been endowed with his mother's qualities of courage, fortitude, and faithfulness. His story reminds us that families inherit good qualities as well as defects. Look for attributes in your ancestors as you research your family history.

The story of the widow Ruth reveals her loving devotion to her husband's mother. When Naomi, recently widowed, left Moab to rejoin her own people in Bethlehem, Ruth's first priority was to care for her mother-in-law. By accompanying the elderly woman on her journey, Ruth unselfishly left behind her own parents and family, along with any hope that she herself might remarry. Even though the Moabites and the Israelites had a common ancestor in Abraham, they were political rivals and enemies.

Ruth, an outsider in Bethlehem, risked abuse and disdain. This did not deter her from working tirelessly in the fields and gathering fallen grain left behind by the harvesters so she could care for Naomi. Her diligence and family loyalty won her the protection and admiration of Boaz, and eventually they married. (Book of Ruth)

Are there similar examples of family devotion and self-sacrifice in your family's history?

Ruth's son, Obed, was the grandfather of the shepherd boy, David, who bravely slew the giant Goliath. Later, as King David, he secured the City of David (Jerusalem) as the Israelite capital. David is celebrated as a brilliant leader, statesman, musician, poet, and psalmist. A religious man, he was respected and loved for his virtues, in spite of his faults and weaknesses.[2] His story is told in the Books of Samuel.

David angered Yahweh by conspiring to kill Uriah after sleeping with the soldier's wife, Bathsheba. David fasted in remorse but his first child, who was born from that illicit relationship, died a few days after its birth.

In spite of his successful conquests as King and the many children born to his wives, David's household suffered a large portion of grief. His beautiful daughter Tamar was raped by his son, Amnon, an event that so angered her brother Absalom, he murdered his half-brother Amnon.

As the thirdborn son, Absalom's motives may have been tainted by ambition. He became heir to his father's throne upon the death of Amnon. Although he eventually reconciled with his father, he cunningly seduced people to abandon their loyalty to the King. Rivalry with his father finally ended in Absalom's death while leading a rebellion against his father's army. His death deeply grieved David.

The kingdom of David was troubled with division, family discord, and insurrection. His lust for women was apparently inherited by Amnon, and David's murder of Uriah was echoed in the murders of his own sons.

David's story is interesting because it is also the ancestral story of Jesus. Jesus understands family division and brokenness. The Messiah who redeemed us by paying the ultimate price for our sins descended from the dysfunctional House of David. (Mt 1:1-17; Lk 3:23-38) It is through Jesus' sacrifice and death for all men's sins that we appeal to Yahweh for a healing of our own bloodlines.

You are encouraged to find the Bible stories that best describe your ancestors. Your study of Scripture will enlighten your mind as it helps you resolve your family history questions. Every family has dark pages in the chapters of its stories and Jesus knows the sadness and the strife you and your ancestors have endured. He knows each one's shortcomings but he also sees beyond the defects, recognizing the goodness and the virtues of each one.

WRITE IT ON A TABLET

When the prophet Habakkuk complained about the misery of God's people, Yahweh replied, "...I am doing something in your own days that you would not believe if you were told it." (Hab 1:5) In a vision, God showed the prophet that his prayer was being answered. He told him to write the vision on tablets because the time of fulfillment had not yet come. Those written words served as reassurance of God's promise during the waiting period, and later the fulfillment of those words bore witness to God's faithfulness. (Hab 2:2-3)

Answers to our prayers may require enduring faith and a time of waiting, but we can benefit from Yahweh's advice to Habakkuk. Often, our prayers are being answered without our awareness. Journaling gets us in touch with our thoughts on a deeper level, and helps us to gain new perspectives. The unconscious may have information to share, and writing can provide a release of the ideas and memories that are buried. By writing down our thoughts, we help facilitate the discernment process.

When I first prepared my family tree for healing, I had not yet completed the extensive genealogical research discussed in this book. In fact, I had very little concrete information to guide my prayers, and only a short time available in which to prepare my genogram before the scheduled Mass for our family. I compensated for my incomplete data with an abundance of determination and faith. The Holy Spirit responded generously, recalling forgotten memories to my mind and helping me relate them to the problems of the moment.

As I wrote down facts that I knew, the connections became evident. Daniel L. Schacter reassures us that we don't need all the details of an event in order to emotionally connect the past with the present. He describes memory as a tool that preserves our important beliefs and stores our ties to the past.[3] If you are still having difficulty threading together the data you have gathered about ancestors, try writing their stories.

First, pray to the Holy Spirit for inspiration. Then, beginning with what you know about your ancestor's life and personality, write out that person's story. As an observer to the scene, try to imagine how your ancestor might have felt and reacted in the situations you describe.

If your relative was suddenly stricken with a life-threatening illness, what reaction might you expect? Some people complain loudly and frequently. Others prefer to suffer silently, or in denial.

The response to sudden illness can also be colored by a person's previous experience of illness. The memory of a bad experience can arouse irrational fear. After my father's sudden death from a brief illness, my mother dreaded the emergency room. Even though my father had received expert care there, she blamed the medical staff for his demise. As her own health deteriorated, her apprehension elevated the stress associated with her own illness.

On the other hand, a person whose life has been saved in the emergency room may consider this a place of rescue and survival. You wouldn't have difficulty convincing that survivor of the need for prompt medical care for an emergency health crisis.

Using this approach toward your ancestors and their own varied circumstances, you can begin to envision their lives more clearly. With knowledge comes understanding, and with understanding, compassion.

TWO HEADS ARE BETTER THAN ONE

If you hit a roadblock, seek wise counsel. Discussing your family history questions with someone who has no immediate interest or involvement in your family is another aid to discernment. As you explain the situation you are researching, your listener may provide insights that shed new light on your investigation. The objective comments of an impartial person can bring to mind possibilities you haven't considered.

Perhaps the person you converse with had a similar family experience. Learning how someone else solved a problem can help your discernment. We often think there is only one approach or one solution to every problem. It helps to look at many possible answers and then choose the one that fits best.

We live in a culture that is accustomed to quickly finding answers in books and on the Internet. We also have a natural tendency to measure facts by our own familiar culture. Genealogy research, however, requires you to expand your perspective. You will discover customs and conventions that are totally different from your own.

When I compared my father's Irish birth certificate with other information in the 1901 census for County Mayo, I noticed a major discrepancy. According to the census, both of his parents could read and write in English, but his birth certificate was signed with the mark X. A woman who lives in the area provided a simple and logical explanation. In Ireland long ago, it was not uncommon for births to be registered by someone other than the parents. In order to comply with the civil deadline for registration, the duty might fall upon any neighbor who had business in town, and that person might be illiterate.

As my research continued, I learned that many of the answers I sought were available as local knowledge, information that was not likely to be found in books. Since customs vary from country to country, and even from state to state, do not feel embarrassed about asking questions as you continue your research.

Your family has cultural traditions endemic to its roots. These include everything from favorite foods to philosophy of life. Some cultural traits endure while others fade from sight. Knowledge and perpetuation of your cultural heritage can enhance your family members' appreciation of their roots. Their lives will be enriched by the diversity of tradition handed down to them from past generations.

GOD KNITTED YOU TOGETHER IN THE WOMB

Serious situations call for prompt action. Depending on the urgency of your family's requirement for healing, you may decide not to wait until your ancestral research is complete. Bear in mind that the purpose of your family research is multiple. Any knowledge you gain about your ancestors has the potential to provide insights that will guide your prayers for healing. If, however, your family situation calls for immediate prayer, don't wait. Postpone the in-depth research, compile whatever data you currently have, and proceed with your family tree healing.

Ancestral healing is not magical. It relies on the goodness of God, who is all-knowing as well as all-merciful. God already knows what needs healing. He knows everything about you and your family. The details you obtain in research assist *your* prayer. They help you develop compassion for your ancestors, along with admiration for their positive contributions to your family. These are vital components in family healing, but it is important to maintain a balanced perspective.

Do not worry if your story is incomplete. God is not restricted in any way by your lack of knowledge, just as he is not limited by time and distance. He called you by name, knitted you together in your mother's womb, and knows you through and through. You are his. My lack of details about family history did not prevent the Father from spontaneously healing my daughter's "chronic" schizophrenia.

BURIED TREASURE

Complete your genogram by noting the positive attributes handed down through your family. Who in your family tree displayed creativity? What talents do you and other family members possess?

How were these gifts encouraged by your ancestors? Who in your family demonstrated deep moral integrity? Courage? Loyalty? How did this influence you and other family members? Did any of your ancestors show remarkable strength of character? Often, such a trait results from coping with hardship. How was this characteristic passed on to other family members?

Who experienced a life transformation? A change of lifestyle sometimes occurs in midlife, when a person sets out in a new direction. Perhaps an alcoholic reformed and overcame addiction through a 12-step program. Such determination is to be credited, even though the descendants' lives have already been affected by the drinking behavior. A transformed life is a powerful testimony about strength of character and courage of conviction. This is a valuable legacy for future generations.

Who among your family rebelled against religion, and why? Did any family member make a confession of the past and experience a religious conversion? How were other family members affected or influenced by that decision? Which family member passed the torch of faith to you?

Try to discover each family member's positive attributes. When we can recognize human weakness for what it is, we find it easier to love one another. Our loving acceptance of people just the way they are frees them to grow and become all that they can be. The love in your eyes becomes a bright reflection of Christ's love. Your acceptance says, "You are lovable."

DIVINE WISDOM

All wisdom is from the Lord.... (Eccl 1:1)

Label this section of your notebook: *LOVE AND FORGIVENESS*.

After prayerful contemplation on these questions, spend time writing your answers.

1. Who among your relatives was easy to love?
2. Who was difficult to love?
3. Is there someone that you find difficult to forgive?
4. Have you contributed in any way to family division?
5. What can you do to repair a shattered family relationship?

When you are satisfied with all of your fact-finding efforts, set aside a quiet time and place to prayerfully evaluate all of your data. You will need your notebook and a copy of your genogram. First, call upon the Holy Spirit to help you make good decisions about your family's needs for healing.

Review the pages of your notebook as though you are reading them for the first time. You may receive new insights. Your notations on the genogram will reference specific problems of ancestors or living family members. These symbols will help you identify significant patterns from generation to generation. Try to see beyond any bad decisions that ancestors may have made, and discern the underlying woundedness responsible for their mistakes. (*see* Appendix I)

> *"If we could read the secret history of our enemies, we should find in each man's life sorrow and suffering enough to disarm all hostility."*[4]

Wisdom is a gift and God delights in giving us good gifts. He answers your prayers for discernment so that you will know how best to pray for your family tree. Trust in God's wisdom and providence. You will never know all you would like to know about your ancestors. Be content in knowing that your research was thorough.

Leave the unknown to God. If new information comes to light in the future, you can pray about it then. Family healing is a process.

LORD, INCREASE MY TRUST

Father God, I thank you for your guidance in helping me piece together the many fragments of my family's history. Help me to forgive any transgressions of my ancestors and to love them with a generous heart. Thank you for loving me unconditionally, and for your patience with me when I am shortsighted and impatient. Your process of healing occurs in your perfect timing, Lord, not mine. Jesus, I trust you. Increase my trust. Amen.

Chapter 11.

1. Daniel L. Schacter, "Memory Serves as a Link, Not an Instant Replay," *Los Angeles Times*, August 21, 1996, B9.

2. *Great People of the Bible and How They Lived* (NY, Montreal: Readers Digest Association, Inc., 1974), 164.

3. Daniel L. Schacter. Memory expert and author of *Searching for Memory: The Brain, the Mind, and the Past,* Basic Books.

4. Henry Wadsworth Longfellow; *Driftwood*; 1857.

12. GRAFTING YOUR FAMILY TREE TO THE LORD

"To you, a thousand years are a single day." (Ps 90:4)

The inspiration for a garden often comes from seed catalogs and books that portray beautiful landscapes, but the actual work of gardening requires dedicated labor to realize the dream of the garden in full bloom. Your vision of family healing and wholeness has sustained you through the headwork stage of preparation, as you researched and charted your genogram with prayerful discernment. The second stage requires heartwork.

HEARTWORK

Your new insights about your ancestors have prepared your heart to forgive their failings and to appreciate their positive contributions to your family tree. You have planted the seeds of healing and soon you will experience the fruits of your work.

Tender new growth will languish without proper care. What your family healing requires most at this stage is an outpouring of love and forgiveness. It is difficult to understand and forgive the actions of others. Through your recognition of the circumstances and character flaws that contributed to your ancestors' behavior, compassion is released in your heart. God's healing of your family will be facilitated through your compassionate understanding.

In teaching us how to follow him as Christians, Jesus spoke clearly about love and forgiveness. Our prayers and worship are barren when we harbor unforgiveness in our hearts. If your ancestors' transgressions were gravely serious, you may still find it difficult to move easily from disaffection to forgiveness. When a relative's actions have produced pain in the lives of other family members, it isn't easy to extend pardon. Perhaps you can only raise a trickle of forgiveness for the actions of your ancestor. That is, at least, a beginning.

Each one of us is lovable and forgivable in God's sight. Through his unconditional love, he accepts us just as we are, with our faults and weaknesses. While we may only see the imperfections in one another, our Maker sees the potential in each person. He also understands the woundedness that prevents a person from attaining full potential.

When we try to see others through God's vision, our capacity for love and forgiveness increases. True compassion grows within us when we set aside our prejudices and put on the mind of Christ, who came to redeem all. If you experience difficulty feeling compassion for an ancestor, try to imagine that person as a vulnerable little child. Consider the various aspects of that child's environment. What wounding experiences early in life caused that child to become a flawed adult?

LILACS AND BIRDSONG OR MUD AND MIRE?

An insightful poem describes a child who, as he went forth every day, became the first object that he looked upon. That object also became part of the child—for a day, a portion of a day, or perhaps for "many years or stretching cycles of years." Every day, the child's life was impacted by both positive and negative influences. He experienced early lilacs and birdsong, as well as the mud and mire by the pond. His life was comprised of friendly encounters as well as quarrelsome ones, experiences of acts of meanness as well as of love.[1]

Similarly, your ancestor was shaped by many influences, perhaps by a mother's mildness and a father's manly strength, or by the absence of these qualities. Both wholesome and destructive events shaped the life of the child who would one day pass on a part of that inheritance to you and your family. If your ancestor was unable to give love, there was probably an unmet need for love in his own life. Even if he received love, he may not have perceived the love that was given.

Through your prayers, you can now supply the love that was missing in the lives of ancestors. The healing love of Jesus flows through your compassionate prayers about any events that prevented your relative from reaching full human potential. Because God exists in eternity, not in time, he can heal the past as well as the present. Your forgiveness is the key that opens the door to his healing.

HOW MANY TIMES, LORD?

Jesus told Peter that he must forgive the brother who had wronged him "seventy times seven." (Mt 18:23) How willing are we to forgive someone who has repeatedly hurt us? It may seem easier to love and forgive an ancestor who has died than it is to forgive continual mistreatment by a living family member.

In the parable of the prodigal son (Lk 15:11-32), Jesus spoke to families. This powerful and timeless story involves inheritance, separation, and jealousy—familiar elements in family division. It also contains many elements of healing.

The young man in the story left home and recklessly squandered his inheritance on an immoral lifestyle. When the errant son was finally reduced to total poverty by his wanton way of life, he humbly returned home to beg his father for a lowly job among the servants. He must have been surprised to find his loving father watching and waiting for his return. The father not only welcomed his son with open arms, he ordered a feast to celebrate his homecoming. The prodigal and his father experienced an instantaneous healing of their relationship.

The headstrong son who misused his inheritance represents each of us. When we sin, we squander our "inheritance" and separate ourselves from our Father. Nevertheless, he always welcomes our return with open arms. The Father's joy over our return overshadows any disappointment he may feel about our misbehavior. He loves us unconditionally.

Meanwhile, the faithful and hardworking son was angered by his father's total love and forgiveness of the rebellious younger brother. In contrast with the prodigal son who returned humbled, the dutiful son was proud, judgmental, and self-righteous. He still had much to learn. In spite of his hard work and dedication, he did not merit a reward because he lacked love and compassion.

Mother Teresa said that when the final judgment comes, we will be asked how well we loved. Is there an errant son, daughter, parent or other relative in your family? Do you love them? Can you begin to love them through Christ's love?

The teachings of Jesus are not easy. His message was as radical during his life on earth as it is today. He said that we must all become like little children in order to enter the kingdom of heaven. In the next breath, Jesus said that he came to save those lost sheep that had strayed from the flock. "It is not the will of your Father which is in heaven that one of these little ones should perish." (Mt 18:14) These comments reveal the depth of Jesus' love and concern for the vulnerable and for the wounded.

Jesus, who came to do the will of his Father, surely longs to gather all the lost and tormented souls that are stranded somewhere between heaven and earth. Those who did not complete their soulwork in this life, the separated souls in purgatory, are the souls most in need of our prayers.

SOULWORK

Jesus calls us to a higher standard of love and forgiveness than we might otherwise choose for ourselves. Your prayers for family healing require you to have a generous, Christ-like love for all of your family members, both living and dead. If your forgiveness and reconciliation with a living family member are blocked, apply the technique that helped you love and forgive a deceased ancestor.

Try to imagine your relative as an emotionally wounded child whose needs were not met. Pray for compassionate understanding of what was missing in that person's life, and for the ability to love unconditionally through Christ. Another way to gain appreciation of your relative is to write a brief and objective biography of that person. What positive qualities do others see in your difficult relative? What is it about this person that really eats you up inside?

SHADOWBOXING

Quite often the faults in others that trigger our strong negative reactions are reflections of our own faults. Psychologist Carl Jung called this the shadow element of personality. We often react strongly to those traits in others that we are unable to recognize and own within ourselves. Your soulwork may involve recognizing and accepting your own faults and working on your end of a defective relationship.

Reconciliation is possible when we move from a position of blaming to one of acceptance. Furthermore, by your loving acceptance of the person you find difficult to love, you can become an instrument of healing. Similarly, by embracing both the positive and the negative traits that are part of your own personality, you can begin to love yourself better. This process of self-love leads to improvement in all your relationships, including your relationship with God.

Your research has helped you discern who in your lineage needs prayers for healing. You have recognized patterns or connections between the problems of ancestors and the illnesses or problems of living family members. You have completed your genogram to the best of your ability. With a new heart, you are ready to bring your family to the altar of God.

GETTING TO THE ROOTS OF RELATIONSHIPS

Label this section of your notebook: ***RELATIONSHIPS***.
Ever since Adam and Eve's time, people have struggled with the mystery of God. For a moment, forget what you have been told about him as you explore how you perceive the Father. Words in the list below will help you describe him. Write about your insights.

Loving	Angry	Friend	Truthful
Gentle	Strict	Quiet	Deceptive
Distant	Comforter	Provider	Understanding
Absent	Patient	Thoughtless	Permissive
Impatient	Outgoing	Judgmental	Confidante
Sensitive	Reflective	Savior	Wounded
Teacher	Uncaring	Mean	Approachable
Stingy	Forgiving	Generous	Healer
Friend	Judge	Kind	Authoritarian
Prayerful	Listener	Mediator	Self-centered

1. Do you know Jesus?

2. Which words in the list above describe Jesus for you?

3. Are you seeking Jesus? Where? Are you finding him?

4. Are you hiding from Jesus?

5. When you close your eyes and meditate on the name of Jesus, what image or images enter your mind?

Write about your relationship with Jesus.

Your relationship with your parents can affect the way you relate to God. Reflect upon your childhood. Was it happy? If not, why not? What kind of relationship do you have with your parents today? Do you need healing in those relationships? If so, when did things go wrong in your relationships?

Using words from the list, describe the parents you knew as a child. Describe the parents you know today. Tell Jesus about your hurts, your disappointments, your broken hopes and dreams, and these relationships. Let your inner child express how it feels to suffer those hurts. Then pray in a childlike, imaginative way. Imagine you and your parents holding hands in a circle around Jesus.

ROOTS OF LOVE

Jesus, I know that you love with me with an everlasting love. Thank you for loving me even when I was not aware of your love. Please touch and heal my inner child. Remove all the hurt from the past. I lift up my parents to you. Please heal them of any lack of love they experienced in their own lives. Touch the empty places in their heart with your complete love. Help me to forgive them for the times they were unable to meet my deepest needs. Speak your love into their hearts and spirits. Give us a new beginning, a new relationship with you in the center. Amen.

Chapter 12.

1. Walt Whitman, *Leaves of Grass*, (NY; Signet Classics; New American Library, 1955) 290-291.

Rooted in Jesus

13. GO TO THE ALTAR OF GOD

". . . A peace the world cannot give,
this is my gift to you." (Jn 14:27)

Many people seek healing of their family trees through the celebration of the Eucharistic Liturgy. When we enter into the mystery of Christ in the sacrifice of the Mass, we participate in a celebration that includes the entire Body of Christ, in union with the Trinity, the Godhead. The Mystical Body of Christ includes those who have died, as well as those still living. We bring our prayers for family to God the Father, through Jesus, whose grace is poured out upon us by the Holy Spirit.

Anyone is welcome to attend a Catholic Liturgy and you needn't be Catholic to request a Mass for your special intentions. God's ability to heal your family is not restricted to one form of prayer. All healing flows from his generous mercy towards all of his children. If you feel uncomfortable about participating in the Liturgy, you can use other avenues of prayer for family healing. (*see* Chapter 15)

THE LITURGICAL CELEBRATION

The celebration of the Eucharist is valued by the Catholic Church as the highest form of healing prayer. It is the universal prayer of the Church. By his death on the cross, Jesus paid the greatest price imaginable to redeem us. He suffered and surrendered his life in order to free us from sin. Our participation in the Eucharistic celebration commemorates his death, unites our suffering with his sacrifice, and celebrates his Resurrection gift to us of redemption and new life.

Jesus died to set us free. When we bring our family trees to his holy altar, we ask Jesus to set free our families from the effects of ancestral sin. It is a long-standing custom of the Church to pray for the souls of the dead and any priest can say this Mass for you. Common elements of every Mass include prayers for the living as well as prayers for the deceased. If possible, gather your family together to share in the Liturgy with you. While not required, it is both gratifying and unifying when a family prays together.

BE RECONCILED

The Mass opens with the ancient blessing of the Church, the *Sign of the Cross*. (Mt 28:19) The *Penitential Rite* that follows flows from Jesus' teaching that we must be reconciled with others before we bring our gifts to the altar. (Mt 5:24) We repent and ask pardon for our sins, and for the times we have failed to love. Repent for the times you have failed to love your relatives. Ask pardon for any offenses you may have committed against family members.

As you pray for individual members of your family tree, focus on forgiving those ancestors who are most in need of healing. Ask God's forgiveness of any failings or inability to love on their part, the effects of which may have been passed down through the generations. Since these unhappy souls are unable to speak for themselves, you may apologize to God on their behalf for their transgressions. Pray quietly in your own words or paraphrase the prayer of Jesus as he hung on the cross. You might say, "Father, forgive the transgressions of my ancestors. They knew not what they were doing."

You may also pray that the deceased will forgive you and other family members for any lack of love and understanding towards them. Ask God's healing of any family division that still exists.

Praise and worship is sung or prayed in *The Gloria*, which gives glory to God and asks for peace for his people on earth. Our praise acknowledges the sovereign nature of God and our relationship to him.

The next phase of the Liturgy involves the reading of *Scripture* to enlighten our minds with the word of God. Listen carefully and with an open mind. What is God speaking to you through this sharing of his holy word? His whispers in your heart may inform and guide your prayers.

The *Credo*, or *Creed*, is a summary of the Catholic faith. The words of this prayer restate our belief that Jesus is the Son of God who came to redeem us. He became man and underwent the suffering of the crucifixion to reclaim our birthright as children of God. We acknowledge the Holy Spirit as the person of God who enlightens and inspires, guides and comforts us.

The closing statement of the *Creed* recounts what family healing is all about. We profess our belief in the communion of saints, God's forgiveness of sins, the future resurrection of our bodies, culminating in everlasting life with God. The Church teaches that the communion of saints is comprised of the faithful on earth, the saints in heaven, and the souls in need of purification or healing before entering heaven. We reaffirm our trust in God's forgiveness and anticipate enjoying eternal life with him.

CONSECRATE MY FAMILY, LORD

At the *Offertory*, when the gifts of bread and wine are brought to the altar, present your prayers of petition to the Lord. With the permission of the priest, your genogram may be placed upon the altar as a symbol of your prayers. If that is not possible, keep it with you during the Liturgy.

The priest blesses the gifts, praying that they will be acceptable to God, the Almighty Father. The congregation echoes his prayer in similar words. Then he literally washes his hands, asking the Lord to cleanse him from his sins. Silently ask the Lord to cleanse your family of impurities, to remove any inherited weaknesses of character or health, and to reinforce your family's bond with him.

The *Eucharistic Prayer* begins with a brief exchange of thanksgiving and praise by the celebrant and the congregation. While the priest reads the long prayer of thanksgiving and praise, silently express thanksgiving for the special gifts and blessings you have received from your ancestors, including the gifts of life, of family, and of your faith in God.

The *Sanctus* alerts worshipers that the holiest part of the Mass is at hand. In words or song, the congregation praises God: "Holy, holy, holy, Lord...." The celebrant offers prayers for the entire Body of Christ, mentioning all who are gathered for the Eucharistic sacrifice, and those they hold dear. Mentally add your family members' names at this time and dedicate your family to the Lord.

As the priest calls to mind the saints, apostles, and martyrs of the Church, he asks that we will receive God's constant help and protection through their prayers for us.

BODY AND BLOOD, SOUL AND DIVINITY

The most solemn moment of the Mass has arrived. The Catholic doctrine of transubstantiation teaches that when the celebrant repeats the words uttered by Christ at the Last Supper, the bread and wine are transformed into the real Body and Blood of Jesus. While the substances maintain the appearance of bread and wine after the *Consecration*, they embody the real presence of Jesus.

When the priest consecrates the hosts (wafers of unleavened bread) into the Body of Christ, mentally place your deceased ancestors on the plate with the bread. Ask Jesus to consecrate their lives, to make them whole and holy, and to bring them into full union with him. The priest holds up a large host and solemnly repeats the words of Christ to his disciples at the Last Supper. Inviting them to partake of the Bread of Life, Jesus said "...this is my body which will be given for you." (Lk 22:19)

Next, the celebrant consecrates the wine, transforming it into the blood of Christ and repeating the words of Jesus when he offered it to his disciples. "Drink all of you from this," he said, "for this is my blood, the blood of the (new) covenant which is to be poured out for many for the forgiveness of sins." (Mt: 26:27-28) The new covenant guaranteeing our eternal life with him was sealed by his redemptive sacrifice on the cross. Ask Jesus to cleanse your bloodline, to wash away the effects of sin, and to remove anything that separates your family from him.

The celebrant prays specifically for the *Commemoration of the Dead*, asking that they be brought into the light of God's presence. During these prayers, mentally name the deceased family members you carry in your heart. As you pray for departed relatives, remember especially those who were difficult to love, and those who died suddenly and unexpectedly, without time to prepare their hearts.

Miscarried or unwanted babies may have died unnamed and

without the benefit of Christian burial. It is appropriate at this time to give them an identity by naming them and dedicating them to the Lord.

As the congregation joins hands and prays the words of *The Lord's Prayer*, connect your heart and mind with the words as you speak them. You are recognizing the one true God, paying him honor, acknowledging his sovereignty, trusting in his generosity, forgiving others, and asking for his forgiveness.

One essential element of this prayer asks for God's protection and deliverance from evil. At this time, bring to the Lord any family members who had occult involvement or bondage to evil. Ask God to sever evil attachments once and for all, replacing any spiritually unhealthy attractions with a deep and abiding hunger for his love.

At the invitation to exchange a *Sign of Peace*, you are called to recognize the face of Jesus in those around you and to share his peace and love. It is customary to shake hands with those nearby, saying, "The peace of Christ" or "Peace be with you."

In preparation for *Communion*, the priest affirms that Jesus is the source of salvation and healing. He calls upon the Lamb that was slain for our sins and the congregation joins in, praying aloud, beseeching the Lamb of God who takes away sin to grant us his mercy and peace. Ask him to extend his mercy and peace to your family.

The priest raises a consecrated host, along with the chalice containing the Blood of Jesus, and proclaims to the congregation that this is indeed the Lamb of God who calls us to share in his supper.

With deep faith in the promises of Jesus, respond: "Lord, I am not worthy to receive you, but only say the word and I shall be healed." You speak for your entire family, asking the Lord's healing for living family members, as well as his blessing of peace on your departed ancestors.

COME TO THE LIVING WATER

As this is written, the Catholic Church does not yet share *Com-*

munion with those of other faiths. If you are unable to receive the Eucharist, you may still come forward for a blessing. The correct posture for those who are not receiving is to cross your arms over your chest as you approach the priest or other minister of the Eucharist.

Even if you do not receive the Eucharist physically, you can receive it spiritually, inviting Jesus into your heart at this special moment. As you go forward to receive and welcome Jesus, present yourself on behalf of all generations of your family. Through your union with Jesus, your family is being healed and united.

Communion means joining together, coming into full union with Jesus. This is a time of contemplation. Your prayers have been brought to the Lord's holy altar and he has heard the longings of your heart. Let go of all anxiety. Rest in the presence of the Lord and receive his peace and blessing.

Some people experience visions while praying for their families during this solemn moment. Kenneth McAll described this as an "Afterglow." At one conference, people reported visions of angels, light-filled children, people throwing away dirty clothes, and other symbols of healing.

Once, while praying for unnamed babies that did not survive, I was blessed with the beautiful mental image of a group of baby angels, joyfully dancing in a circle.

During another Liturgy for my family tree, I saw my Irish mother-in-law, Maggie, dancing with a tambourine. She joined Mary Anne, my Irish grandmother, in leading a lively procession of deceased relatives around the room. My father was present with all of his family. As their celebration continued, Maggie jitterbugged with my Dad. Finally, I saw an image of a lake, fed by a current that refreshed the lake and carried away debris. This symbolized the new life God was creating within our family.

The Liturgy closes with a *Blessing* and the celebrant's announcement that the Mass is ended. Be thankful and receive the peace and blessings that only God can give, as you continue to hold your family in your prayers.

The heart of God is loving, compassionate, and forgiving. As he heals the past, he will help you write a bright new chapter for the future.

ARE WE THERE YET?

You may wonder how you will know if your prayers for family healing are being answered? Do not allow anxiety to disturb your newfound peace. Trust in God's mercy and his timing. Continue to pray with an expectant heart and be alert for positive changes in family members. Changes are often noted within a few days after the celebration of a Eucharist for the family.

You will recognize God's healing touch on your family tree when news of healing comes to you. Any positive change of heart is a certain sign that your prayers are being answered. Those alienated from God often experience a spiritual healing or a new openness to the Lord. Troubled relationships show signs of reconciliation. When illness is reversed or improved, the physician will recognize and confirm the healing. Thank God for the healing he has begun and ask him to continue the healing process.

Where you see evidence of a change of heart, pray for the resolve and motivation that person needs to cooperate in the healing process. Spiritual healings need to be rooted and nurtured in a Christian community. All healings call for some element of change or action on the part of those healed.

Read the "Parable of the Sower" (Mt 13:4-9).

Do not be discouraged if you encounter walls of opposition within your family. Change implies risk and many are afraid to take risks. Just remember that a wall turned on its side becomes a bridge.

Bridges carry people safely across obstacles so that they can reach their destination. A bridge must be strong, stable, resilient, and reliable in order to withstand all kinds of weather. New bridges lead people to new destinations, while old restored bridges continue to carry people and their relationships forward.

You are leading family members over a bridge to healing. You cannot force anyone to cross the bridge if they are unwilling or unready, but with patience, tolerance, and prayer, you can be an encourager.

LORD, GRANT YOUR PEACE

Father, I thank you for the many ways you are blessing my family tree. Deepen my faith and my trust as I wait for your miracles to unfold. Surround my family members with angelic protection and keep their hearts open to the healing you are doing in their lives. Grant all of us the motivation to accept and cooperate with your grace, so that we can be one family in you, Lord. Amen.

14. WRITE A NEW CHAPTER

*"Make our future as happy
as our past was sad..."* (Ps 90:15)

There are numerous varieties of families, just as there are many kinds of gardens. When we are very young, we accept our own family as the norm. Then, as our circle of friends and acquaintances widens through school and outside activities, we begin to realize that other families are different from ours.

There are no perfect families. Parents do the best they can at the time, given their gifts and their circumstances. You as a parent have done the best you can. Generational healing helps us to move out of self-pity and to move on. God can bring good out of our mistakes. (Rom 8:28) Rather than looking back with regret at the mistakes you have made, look ahead. Begin today to write a new chapter in your family's history.

EXPECT MIRACLES

When I began my quest for family healing in 1985, my principal concern was for my daughter, who for six years had been lost in a world of chronic schizophrenia. After Father Hampsch celebrated a Liturgy for our family tree, her mental condition improved dramatically overnight. Her disruptive voices, suicidal inclinations, and racing thoughts disappeared. Her most serious problem had been healed. The next day, she reported this dream:

"I saw Jesus beckoning to me from across a green meadow. In the meadow were colorful flowers, many animals, birds, bees and butterflies (*all symbols of fertile growth and new life*). I bounded over to Jesus gracefully and he embraced me. He told me not to be afraid, that he was with me always, and I must follow him."

Several days later, an evil voice returned, urging my daughter to end her life. She quickly banished it by praying the simple deliverance I had taught her. Within two weeks of the Mass said by Father Hampsch, my daughter's caregivers recognized her improvement and began planning for her discharge to a less-restrictive facility. Within a few months, her doctor reduced her psychotropic medication by one-half. Meanwhile there were reports of healing from other family members.

Several men in the family reported feeling that something indefinable had been lifted from them. They experienced a new sense of peace. I personally experienced healing of a long-troubled family relationship.

At that time, one son was involved in a civil lawsuit over serious injuries he had incurred in an automobile accident. The injuries had ended his Navy career. The day after our Mass for the family tree, his lawyer took the final deposition in preparation for litigation over my son's injuries. What happened was extraordinary!

Anxious to "get a burden off his chest," one of the defendants voluntarily admitted to my son's attorney that he and his companion had been drinking the night of the accident. He confessed that his friend had caused the accident when she ran a red light and broadsided the car in which my son was a passenger. Needless to say, the court ruled in my son's favor and the resulting settlement helped him rebuild his life.

Since this deposition was taken the very next day after our Mass for the family tree, I do not believe this was a coincidence. Such an admission of guilt by a defendant to the plaintiff's attorney is highly unusual. God's power is unlimited. Even though I did not specifically ask for God's intervention in the lawsuit, God read my heart and knew my deep concern. He is a God of surprises who provides for all of our needs. When we are truly open to his healing in our lives, he can accomplish more than we ever dreamed possible.[1]

PLANT A HEDGE OF LOVE

What if your prayers for family healing appear to remain unanswered? Deep healing is a process and the results are not always immediately visible. Some gardens have suffered so much neglect they are overgrown with thorns and nettles and surrounded by broken walls. (Prov 24:30-31) Renovation may require hauling away enormous piles of emotional rubble, pulling out thorny hedges of anger by the roots, and replacing crumbling walls with a hedge of love firmly planted around your family.

Healing the brokenness of family members is complex because the grace of healing poured out upon them requires their cooperation. This is especially true in cases of addictive behavior, family relationship problems, problems related to demonic involvement, and even some physical and mental illnesses.

Following a Mass for generational healing, a family member may announce a new decision to seek help for alcoholism, and may even decide to participate in a 12-step program. If this change of heart proves temporary, it does not mean that God's healing grace has failed. Rather the person is unable to act on the grace. That person may not yet be strong enough to let go of alcohol dependency. The operative word is *yet*!

The healing may require more prayer, along with further action on the part of the addict. Habits are difficult to break and many addictions have roots in buried pain. People whose lives are controlled by addiction need prayers for increased self-motivation. You can also pray for continued enlightenment about the root causes of the addiction, so that your prayer can be more effective.

The healing of broken relationships requires a softening of hearts and attitudes in everyone involved. In other words, the grace for healing also requires forgiveness and apology on the part of people who are estranged. If this is not possible, there can still be healing within those who cooperate with God's grace, and their ongoing prayers can soften hearts and restore relationships to complete reconciliation.

Any improvement in a family member's health after prayers for your family tree is a sign that healing has begun. It is important for your relative to change unhealthy lifestyle habits and to follow the physician's advice. Again, you can pray for the grace of motivation so that your relative will cooperate with the healing. It is unreasonable to expect Jesus to heal our diseases if we refuse to take necessary medicines, eat sensibly, exercise, and follow the basic guidelines for good health.

When a family member with mental illness shows spontaneous improvement after generational healing, be encouraged. In their books, John Hampsch, C.M.F. and Dr. Kenneth McAll have described cases involving complete cures of psychotic conditions through generational healing.

Sometimes there are multiple layers of mental problems. If only a partial healing occurs, give thanks for the improvement. Meanwhile, continue to "soak" the person in prayer, asking God to remove every trace of mental dysfunction. Ask him to provide everything your relative needs to live a normal and independent life.

SPIRITUAL ARMOR

The healing of attachments to the occult and evil requires a complete resolve to avoid future contamination. Once that door is closed, it must remain closed. The person whose life has been invaded by demonic forces may need deep cleansing prayer from someone experienced in this area. Jesus freely gives the grace for healing demonic bondage when we pray for it. You can be certain, however, that the enemy does not retreat willingly. A master of deception, he will try to regain his foothold in a person's life.

One priest, teaching about deliverance from evil spirits, explained, "After you get rid of the rats, you have to plug up all the holes so they can't return." If the void isn't filled with positive and life-giving influences, the negative and destructive forces find it easy to return. Renouncing evil is only part of the healing process. A close relationship with Jesus is essential. Healing requires distancing oneself from companions who delve in occult practices. Disposal of all books and other items that have occult connections is essential. Sources of temptation must be eliminated. Without changes, there is grave danger of falling back into the realm of evil.

A person who has been in bondage to evil needs ongoing prayers for protection. St. Paul counsels us to gird for battle against the forces of darkness. God's spiritual armor consists of truth, integrity, the gospel of peace, faith and salvation, and the word of God for a sword. (Eph 6:10-17)

If spiritual warfare erupts, a simple prayer of deliverance can be said, such as: "Lord Jesus, I bind this spirit of …and command it to leave, in your name. Praise you, Jesus. Thank you, Jesus." Send the spirit to the feet of Jesus for disposal, so that it cannot harm another. You can pray for deliverance for yourself, and also on behalf of your loved ones, when you discern the need for it.

Positive actions that offer protection against backsliding include: frequent participation in the Eucharist, a prayerful life, involvement in a Christian community, and Scripture study. Prayers for angelic protection are helpful, especially in times of temptation. Call upon St. Michael the Archangel and his legions of angels for assistance.

HOLY WISDOM

Generational healing removes negative encumbrances handed down through the lineage. Nevertheless, your children and their children will still encounter problems in their lives. Ancestral healing is not a magical cure-all. Life continues to present new challenges and difficulties.

Healing of my family tree helped me realize that God did not want me to personally carry all the burdens of other family members. Rather I was to help them carry their own burdens by offering love and support. This was a valuable lesson in letting go. By surrendering family problems to God, I was not abandoning my responsibility to my family. I was not reneging on my love for them. Rather, I was entrusting them to the love of the Father, who knows what is best for each of his children.

Upon long reflection, I realized that the troubled environment of my childhood caused me to develop necessary strengths and helped me to become the person God intended me to be. Because I grew up with wounded parents, I learned survival skills. When I had special needs that could not be met at home, God sent wise people into my life to guide me. What I finally realized is that God gave me just the parents I needed.

God imparts wisdom when we quiet our minds and listen. Long after our first family tree healing, I was still struggling with a difficult relationship. Finally, while making my confession at a contemplative retreat, I shared about my problems with a family member whose negativity and bitterness created enormous tension in our relationship. My obsession with the problem was destroying my peace of mind.

The priest counseled me to surround this difficult person with love and to pray for her every day. He advised me to have true repentance for my own sinfulness in this relationship, and to ask God to release her from depression and negativity. Furthermore, I was to hold her in light and love.

Puzzled, I wondered how I could accomplish this. As I prayerfully thought about the priest's advice, the Lord explained it to me. My constant complaints were sowing additional seeds of bitterness around the relationship. In order to have healing, I needed to let go of bitterness and sow love all around her. Humbled, I asked God to help me understand, and to give me the grace necessary to change my attitude. Later in the retreat, the Lord met me at the source of my conflict.

During a service for the Healing of Memories, Jesus showed me where the first tendrils of bitterness had been planted. Over the years, bitterness had become firmly rooted deep within me, concealed from my awareness. I needed to pull out bitterness by the roots—those tenacious roots that were enabling it to thrive and to crowd out love and goodness.

The truth was so clear I could no longer ignore it. I was the only one who could change this problem relationship. It had very little to do with the other person. It was so humbling for me to realize that I had been responsible for my own misery in this situation.

When Jesus shines his light into dark corners of the soul and opens our hearts to the truth, the impossible becomes possible.

On the quest for family healing, you find yourself confronted with the truth: healing begins with you. Healing of your family's brokenness includes an admission of your own woundedness and your own failings. If the only healing you experience is a new awareness of your own imperfection, the journey can be counted as a success. The healing you receive will radiate to those around you, to all who are involved in your life.

We all long to change others but the truth is that we can only change ourselves. As we change and grow, our relationships with others change. They, in turn, have the opportunity to change and grow. When we invite Jesus into our relationships, we give him freedom to act within them.

GOD'S PERFECT TIMING

Do not be discouraged if your prayers did not result in the answers you expected. Acknowledge that God's timing may not be your timing. Continue to pray and in the meantime, create an environment in which family members are fully appreciated for their true selves. Learn to love as Jesus does, unconditionally.

If your prayers about complex problems appear unanswered, it doesn't mean that God has closed the door.

Frequently, our prayers for healing are being answered without our knowledge. God always heals in some way when we pray for healing.

Your prayers for family healing have necessarily focused a great deal of attention on the past. For healing to be complete, however, you must also address attitudes and behaviors in the present.

Jesus told us to love our neighbors as we love ourselves. He didn't say, "Love only the people you choose to love." That is like saying, "Brush only the teeth you want to keep." The teeth you don't care for will decay and rot. Relationships deprived of love and nurturing suffer a similar fate.

Your family has a new beginning, a clean slate. Along with writing a new chapter for future generations, why not develop a plan to avert future family division and brokenness. Love is the glue that keeps a family intact. With informed love as the common denominator, you can avert the mistakes made by past generations.

Just as hearts need to soften to repair damaged relationships, there is much that can be done to prevent future brokenness. Attitudes begin as small opinions but they grow into habits. The seeds of today's attitudes become tomorrow's prejudices and intolerance.

Using what you know about your ancestors, you can learn from the past and avoid the mistakes they made. Nature abhors a vacuum. Fill all the nooks and crannies that were emptied of destructive attitudes and behaviors with the love of Jesus.

Keep a prayerful watch over your family and remain open to new information. In the weeks and months that follow, you may receive fresh insights into your family history. These can be taken to the Lord with ongoing healing prayer. God's covenant promised blessings to a thousand generations for those who love him. Root your family in Jesus and reap the blessings that were promised.

ROOTED IN JESUS

Children learn what they live. They learn to love and trust God when this is modeled for them within their families. Pope John Paul II described the family unit as, "...the school of life where the tension between independence and communion, unity and diversity are lived out on a unique and primary level."[2] Parents must teach moral values and live virtuous lives because children need good role models.

Children also need freedom to make mistakes. Mistakes can be springboards to growth. Their mistakes can teach them they are lovable and forgivable, even when they blunder. Children develop responsibility when they realize that their actions have consequences.

There is a delicate balance between teaching children and controlling their lives. Parents need the wisdom to know when to step back and allow maturing children to solve their own problems. Without that skill, they will be incapable of solving problems in adulthood.

We truly love our family members when we stop trying to control their lives. This is especially true with adult children. When we set one another free, we allow others the dignity and freedom to work through their difficulties and to discover God's plan for their lives. Deep peace flows from the recognition that God is in control.

The Holy Father frequently emphasizes the dignity of marriage and the family. "Was it not through a family, the family of Nazareth, that the Son of God chose to enter into human history?"[3] That fact alone reminds us that God favors the family structure he created.

It is within the framework of family that many of life's important lessons are learned. It is there that children's values are formed. Today's children become tomorrow's ancestors. An investment in the quality and spirituality of family life now will yield abundant blessings for the generations that follow.

When life presents new problems and you are faced with difficult choices, keep your eyes focused on Jesus. Pray to the Holy Spirit before making difficult decisions and follow the advice of St. Paul:

> You must live your whole life according to the Christ you have received—Jesus the Lord; you must be rooted in him and built on him and held firm by the faith you have been taught, and full of thanksgiving. Make sure that no one traps you and deprives you of your freedom by some secondhand, empty, rational philosophy based on the principles of this world instead of on Christ. (Col 2:6-8)

FAMILY REUNION

*"When the whole family is together,
the soul is in place."* (Russian proverb)

Label this section of your notebook: **A NEW BEGINNING.**

1.   In what ways is the Lord asking you to be more loving to those within your family?

2.   What help do you need from him to accomplish this?

3.   Why not ask him for help right now?

Family healing creates an environment in which members can grow strong, unified and morally healthy. Families that are strong and healthy are building blocks for a strong and healthy world.

Read: Is 55:12-13.
"All the trees of the countryside clap their hands." Rejoice as God transforms your thorn bushes into cypress, and your briar patches into fragrant myrtle.

Celebrate the unique story of your family, which has value beyond measure. It is a story of birth and death, hopes and dreams, laughter and tears, successes and disappointments, healing and brokenness, love and ambivalence, saints and sinners, reconciliation and woundedness.

Consider writing a story about your family that will provide your heirs with a sense of their roots. Children need a sense of the past to guide their steps into the future. The story of their ancestors is a gift they will treasure and pass on to their children.

The Lord sets very high standards for us. We may think they are too high, or perhaps we fail to understand what he is asking. Know this. When we say "yes" to the Lord, he provides everything we need. God never assigns a task without providing the necessary tools.

LORD, WE ARE YOUR NEW CREATION

Heavenly Father, I celebrate your gift of family. You have unshackled us from the mistakes of the past and created us anew. You have rooted out old patterns of brokenness, sinfulness, unforgiveness, bondage, and idolatry. Nurture within us peace, goodness, forgiveness, freedom, and surrender to you, Lord. Help us to write a beautiful new chapter for our descendants as we walk with Jesus through all of our tomorrows. Amen.

Chapter 14.

1. *The Jesus Walk: The Road to Healing Body and Soul*, 142-146.

2. John Paul II, Message to the United Nations, March 19, 1994. In "A Spirituality for Families for the Third Millennium," by Cardinal Adam Maida, *Columbia*, October 1996, 11.

3. John Paul II, Apostolic Letter: "As the Third Millennium Draws Near" (Tertio Millennio Adveniente), 28.

Rooted in Jesus

15. THE LIGHT IN THE GARDEN

"I am with you always..." (Mt 28:20)

In the process of photosynthesis, energy from the sun is absorbed and transformed into life-sustaining organic compounds. The transforming energy of light, a basic requirement for life, is essential to the health of a garden. Similarly, a healthy family tree requires light. Ancestral bondage functions in the dark, operating unseen and often unrecognized by those who are suffering. In the process of family tree healing, Jesus illuminates the darkness and heals the effects of our ancestors' transgressions. The light that heals your family tree is also the light that ensures life and protects it.

It is important for the family to strengthen its life-sustaining bond with Jesus, the source of light and healing. Without his help, family members can easily slip back into old behaviors and habits that previously kept them in chains.

CONTINUED HEALING

Now that you have given your family problems to the Lord for his healing, trust that your prayer has been heard. You can continue to pray for your family each time you participate in the Liturgy. As new information is revealed, you can request another Mass with prayer focused on the newly discovered family issues. In the meantime, pray that family members will walk in the light of Jesus. Pray that they will be motivated to cooperate with the healing Jesus has begun in their lives. Pray that your children will stay close to Jesus throughout their lives, a blessing they will pass on to future generations.

HONOR THY FAMILY

Learn to be creative in your prayers for family healing. Begin with some of the suggestions that follow and you will soon find other ways to fit family prayer into your busy routine. The Eucharistic Liturgy is considered by many to be the perfect prayer for family healing. A detailed explanation of the Liturgy can be found in the *Catechism of the Catholic Church.* The elements that comprise the Liturgy can be included in your family's daily routine.

The Eucharistic Liturgy includes: praise and worship, repentance, readings from Scripture, prayers of petition for the living and the dead, transubstantiation of bread and wine into the Body and Blood of Christ, communion with the redemptive sacrifice of Jesus on the cross, and prayers of thanksgiving and blessing.

Upon awakening in the morning, offer a prayer of praise and worship to God. Ask him to bless and protect your family throughout the day and encourage your family members to start each day with this prayer.

Every family meal can be reverenced as "family communion," a sacred time that family members share together. In a loving and congenial atmosphere, you can learn about one another's activities and concerns. The traditional prayer of thanksgiving before meals provides a wonderful opportunity to pray together as a family. Each member can be encouraged to express gratitude for some little blessing of the day. Grace before meals can include a brief prayer for family unity and healing. You might say, "Father, we thank you for the gift of family. We thank you for those who walked the path before us, for those who walk with us, and for those who will follow. Bless us and heal us."

When time permits, perhaps on the weekend, you could include a brief Scripture reading before your family's main meal together. This can provide a topic for meaningful discussion during the meal.

Consider sharing a short family prayer after the meal, during which family members can petition God with any concerns or needs of family members and friends. This simple prayer is a fitting conclusion to the "family communion" and will be a source of blessing and encouragement for each one.

Make repentance a part of family life by teaching your children to reflect on the ways they have caused hurt to another and to be truly sorry. With your help, the words "I'm sorry" will have depth and sincerity. An appropriate time for reflections and repentance is at bedtime. Never allow the sun to set on family anger.

One way you can foster repentance is to model it in your own life. Take time to explain to your children that you are sorry for losing your temper, for hurting their feelings, or for using words that were harsh and critical. Give them an opportunity to forgive you.

YOUR FATHER KNOWS YOUR NEEDS

For those who want ongoing prayer for family healing, and for those who are not comfortable participating in the Liturgy, there are other ways to pray.

Jesus said, "...your Father knows what you need before you ask him." (Mt 6:8) Read Mt 6:7-15, in which Jesus teaches "The Lord's Prayer." Pray this prayer for your ancestors with conscious deliberation, meditating on the meanings of the words:

"Our Father, who art in heaven, hallowed be thy name." We acknowledge God as the one and true God, the only one deserving of our praise and allegiance. This is our response to the Lord's first commandment. (Ex 20:5)

"Thy kingdom come, thy will be done, on earth as it is in heaven." We recognize the sovereignty of God and we align our will with his, trusting in his fairness and love for each one of us.

"Give us this day our daily bread..." Again, we rely solely on God's generosity, the Father whose love is unconditional and everlasting.

"...and forgive us our trespasses," We ask for God's perfect forgiveness for the times we have turned away from him through sin, for the times we have failed to love, for the times that our sins have hurt our family. We also ask, on behalf of our deceased ancestors, for his forgiveness of their shortcomings, their failures and their sins.

"...as we forgive those who trespass against us." We ask the Lord to grant us forgiving hearts, so that we may forgive others through *his* love and compassion. Feelings are simply emotions over which we have no control. They come unbidden and they leave. What matters most is how we act on our feelings. Free will

allows us to choose virtue over recrimination. Whether or not we *feel* forgiving in the present moment, we now make an act of the will to forgive through divine forgiveness.

"Lead us not into temptation, but deliver us from evil." We call upon God to guide us on his path of goodness and sanctity, to free us from the bonds of evil, and to protect us from evil inclinations in the future. We ask this on behalf of our ancestors, our living family, and ourselves.

"Amen." So be it. We pray with the assurance that our prayer is heard by God and answered in a loving way.

JOURNALING PRAYER

Consider writing your own meditation on *The Lord's Prayer,* tailoring sections of the prayer to your family's special needs. When praying for someone who lacks faith, meditate on the opening lines. As you pray for daily bread, meditate on the family member who fails to provide for his family's needs, or the one who is impoverished. When you ask for forgiveness, include broken relationships. The words that ask protection from temptation can address addictions and other weaknesses. Finally, when you pray for deliverance, keep in mind those battling with sinful inclinations.

Writing prayers in your own words helps you focus your prayer. You may want to use your written prayer on a daily basis. Try writing other simple prayers.

TWO OR THREE GATHERED IN HIS NAME

Jesus promised that wherever two or more gather together for prayer, he is with them. Consider asking family members to form a prayer chain. With a simple phone list, the prayer requests can quickly be passed from one family member to another. If all of the members have Internet access, the prayer intentions can be quickly sent by e-mail. Families that are geographically separated could participate in a family chat room on the Web. The idea is to storm heaven with prayers.

Family members might be interested in forming a circle of

prayer that meets regularly to share family concerns. Each one could draw the name of another and pray for that person's needs during the week. Friends and neighbors who have family concerns might be willing to meet once a week for prayer. It is important, in these little prayer groups, to respect one another's privacy by keeping sharings confidential. The faith of the group is built up when members share about the ways the prayers have been answered.

THOUSANDS OF BLESSINGS

Yahweh promised thousands of blessings upon those who love him and keep his commandments. (Ex 20:5-6)You may be the only person in your family with a concern for ancestral healing. Once I asked, "Lord, why do I have to carry the burden for so many family members?" And he answered, "Because I also gave you the strength, the faith, and the necessary gifts, so that you can help them." Accept your task as a blessing from God.

> You will rebuild the ancient ruins,
> build up on the old foundations,
> You will be called Breach-mender,
> Restorer of ruined houses.   (Is 58:12)

It is easy to become so preoccupied with one's problems that the blessings are overlooked. Continue to look for the blessings in your family. Who was the nurturer in your family? Who affirmed you and encouraged you? Who, in your family, inspired your deep concern for family healing? No matter how many problems your family endures, you can recognize numerous reasons to be thankful.

Don't just look for blessings. Claim them on behalf of your entire family. They are your rightful inheritance as a child of the Father, redeemed by Jesus, and filled with gifts by the Holy Spirit.

> In your offspring all the families of
> the earth shall be blessed. (Acts 3:25)

REMEMBERING

Think of ways to honor your ancestors.

1.   Make a prayer tree. Pot a tree branch in sand. Tie on tags with family names as a reminder to pray for them.

2.   Celebrate family generations with photo albums, collage frames, and scrapbooks that you share with the family.

3.   Keep a memento of a family member in a prominent place, as a reminder to pray for them.

4.   Create a small shrine with an ancestor's photo and a crucifix.

5.   Make a family visit to the cemetery to pray for the ancestors buried there. Encourage children to pray for deceased ancestors.

6.   On the anniversary of an ancestor's birthday, have a family celebration. As you memorialize the person, bless them with the gifts that they needed in life, such as faith, hope, courage, gentleness, cheerfulness, perseverance, and generosity.

7.   Rewrite history. Write a brief story of an ancestor's life as it was. Then rewrite it as it might have been had they been healed.

8.   Make a Family Timeline. Have each member write down dates, along with comments about significant events. Pray about these as a group.

9.   Place a large map on the wall and add the names and dates of family members on the places where they lived.

10. Plant a tree in honor of the family. Make this an occasion for celebration.

Read Is 58:6-12.

THE HEALING GARDEN

Relax, close your eyes, and meditate. Imagine a lovely garden warmed by rays of sunshine in the daytime and illuminated by moonbeams and starlight at night. Evening clouds edged with brightness pass over and raindrops fall gently upon the rich soil.

Gentle breezes freshen the air, disseminating the fragrance of flowers and healing herbs. This is a place of rest and repose. When you pray here, God touches your soul. What do you tell God about your family tree? What does God say to you?

JESUS, WE WANT TO WALK WITH YOU

Father God, shine your light of love on my ancestors and on my living family, so that I may recognize all of their merits and goodness. Help me to see them as you do, with the potential to become all that they can be. Lord Jesus, you have walked with all generations of my family. May we continue to walk with you all the days of our lives, until we live in eternity with you. Amen.

Rooted in Jesus

AN AFTERWORD

A ncient trees are encoded with unseen attributes that define the growth of young trees. An oak tree does not bear apples. As you look back on the lives of your ancestors, you will understand the ways your ancestors' traits, attitudes, and actions played a significant role in shaping your life. What you do with the raw material is up to you.

A garden is a place of growth and new life. In retrospect, I realize that I learned life's biggest lessons during the difficult times in my life. God blessed me with family members and circumstances that forced me to grow, much the way a spring bulb can be forced to bloom in the dark of winter.

Today, I thank God for the difficult times and for the lessons he was striving to teach me. I was not an easy case and I surely would have taught God patience, if such a thing were possible. Wherever you are in your relationships, trust God's underlying wisdom in the lessons he is offering you. Someday you will understand where God was leading you and why things happened the way they did.

A BLESSING

May you always find the rainbows hidden behind the dark clouds in your life. May your storms be transformed into soft rains, and may your worries be carried away by gentle breezes. May God lift your burdens and fill your heart with joy as he heals your family tree. Above all, may you be blessed with patience as you wait and watch faithfully for flowers in your family garden.

I WATCH

Faithful I keep my daily watch
as stems grow tall
and buds begin to form.

An unrelenting midwife
to the growing thing,
I'm there each morn.

And when at last
the leaves unfold
and bring

A showy blossom—
disregarding calendars
I welcome Spring.

—Patricia A. McLaughlin

APPENDIX 1. GARDENING TOOLS

CHECKLISTS OF FAMILY TRAITS AND PATTERNS

In the discernment process, be alert for family defects passed down through the generations. These include: spiritual, physical, emotional, relational and societal defects. Following are some examples of family traits and patterns to look for. These lists, while not all-inclusive, will help your discernment. Add other traits that apply to your family.

POSITIVE TRAITS: love; kindness; concern; compassion; faith; faithfulness; spirituality; creativity; talents and gifts; faith; religious convictions; integrity; happiness; moral values; courage; loyalty; strength of character; constancy; honesty; intelligence; life transformation; religious conversion; resilience; perseverance; sense of responsibility; gentleness; nurturing; generosity; diligence; industrious; prudence; wisdom; sincerity; strong principles, self-discipline; education; intelligence; sense of humor.

NEGATIVE TRAITS OR PATTERNS:

Abusive Behavior: child abuse; verbal abuse; wife battering; elder abuse or battering; rape; sexual abuse; molestation. (Some people bury unpleasant happenings. Memories of violation often return at midlife or later. Molestation is reported to be a root cause, though not the only cause, of low self-esteem and eating disorders.)

Accidents and Traumatic Deaths: death by accidents of any kind (drownings, fires, automobile, airplane, ships, industrial); accident prone; suicide; murder; assisted death; sudden or violent death (such as choking on food).

Addictions: alcoholism; gambling; smoking; sexual addiction or deviations; pornography; workaholism; Internet; shopping; illegal drug or substances; medications (common in older people); co-dependency; religious fanaticism.

Attitudes and Weaknesses: moral weakness; immorality; judgmentalism; pessimism; negativity; gossiping; backbiting; anger; rage; bitterness; despair; selfishness; resentment; self-centeredness; greed; jealousy; pride; envy; lust; laziness; poor judgment; self-defeating behavior; deception; self-pity; miserliness; bias; prejudice; sexism; revenge; disrespect; bigotry; discrimination; gender bias; rudeness; stuttering; contentiousness; victim mentality; attitude of superiority; communication problems.

Antisocial Behavior: reclusion; eccentricity; shoplifting; fraud; criminal behavior; grave sinfulness; gang membership; mafia; violence.

Bondage: Relationships that take over and control a person's life: co-dependency; unhealthy attachment to the living or the dead; unfinished grief. Attitudes and obsessions: stereotypes; the past; sin; occult; fear; demonic spirits. Bondage to things includes: money; materialism; anything that is valued more than one's relationship with God or with family and friends.

Eating Disorders: obesity; anorexia; bulimia; excessive exercise; gluttony.

Homosexuality: gender confusion; homosexual or lesbian lifestyle.

Infant Deaths: miscarriages; stillbirths; early deaths; crib deaths; abortions. Post-abortion syndrome is a latent result of abortion. When the guilt and self-hatred surface, the need for forgiveness and reconciliation with God are imperative. Others who may be affected by the death of uncommitted babies (those unbaptized and/or who did not receive a Christian burial) are: siblings, especially the next-born child; the most sensitive child in the family; a twin of the deceased child; a child who survived abortion; a child adopted or conceived to replace the baby who died; fathers; grandparents.

Mental or Emotional Disorders: developmental handicap; autism; schizophrenia; voices; paranoia; clinical depression; hysteria; anxiety; neurotic behavior; irrational or bizarre behavior; suicidal tendencies; delusions of grandeur (thinking they are Jesus or some famous person); extreme nervousness; violent behavior; self-destructive behavior; regression (temper tantrums; thumbsucking); excessive sleeping; phobias (such as: agoraphobia, claustrophobia, fear of heights, water etc.); obsessive or compulsive behavior; anxiety; neurotic guilt; narcissism; shell shock; post-traumatic syndrome.

Occult Involvement: astrology; Ouija boards; certain fantasy role-playing games; fortune telling; palm reading; tea reading; divination; seances; New Age practices and beliefs; crystals; tarot cards; transcendental meditation; witchcraft; curses; curanderos; santeria (Afro-Cuban polytheistic practice of spiritualism); satanism.

Physical Illness: cancer; cardiovascular disease; migraine events; back problems; arthritis; diabetes; epilepsy; AIDS; asthma; respiratory disorders; cystic fibrosis; ulcers; Alzheimer's; senile dementia; eye disorders; birth defects; physical handicaps; neurological disease; fibromyalgia; any illness that does not respond to normal medical treatment; hypochondriasis; death wish; a spirit of infirmity (a tendency to be sick all the time).

Relationships: parent-child issues; mentors; godparents; family feuds; unforgiveness; grudges; infidelity; separation; divorce; uncommitted relationships; adultery; siblings; step-families; adoptions; foster parents; black sheep; family secrets; isolation; estrangement; incest; family secrets; out-of-wedlock births; abandonment issues.

Spiritual Problems: atheism; agnosticism; fallen away from religion; unresolved anger with God; polytheism, cults; unrepented sin.

Rooted in Jesus

YOUR GENOGRAM

A genogram is a family tree (pedigree) chart with symbols added. Charting your ancestors' names and data helps you organize the information in a logical way. The addition of symbols or key words relating to significant events in each person's life yields a shorthand language that helps you identify patterns in your lineage.

Working from the data in your research notebook, draw a diagram with your name and birth date. Add the names of your parents with their dates of birth, marriage, and death if applicable. Include place of birth and emigration dates, if known. Then add the same data for your maternal and paternal grandparents, and for their parents. You now have four generations of your family charted. (*see* Figure 1. Genogram)

If you are married or have been, make a similar chart for your spouse.

A separate descendants' chart will show your marriage and will include all of your children, as well as any grandchildren and great-grandchildren. As the work expands, you can make separate genograms showing brothers and sisters, aunts and uncles, and cousins. The size of your family determines the number of charts. If there have been remarriages or adoptions, you will need to show those connections as well.

Figure 1. Genogram

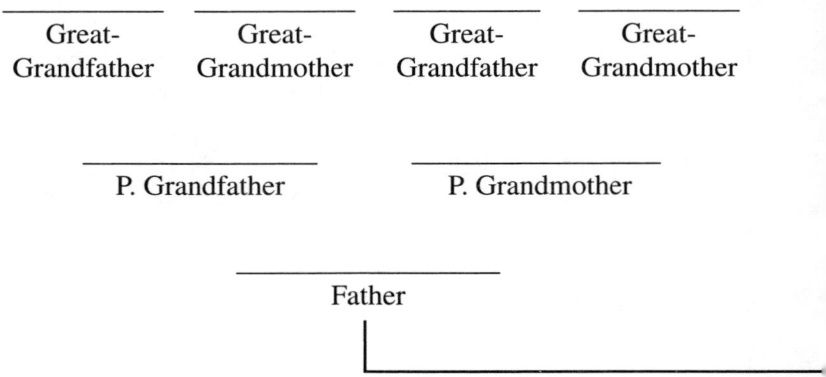

| Great-Grandfather | Great-Grandmother | Great-Grandfather | Great-Grandmother |

| P. Grandfather | P. Grandmother |

Father

4 GENERATION ASCENDANT GENOGRAM

Great-Grandfather	Great-Grandmother	Great-Grandfather	Great-Grandmother

M. Grandfather   M. Grandmother

Mother

YOU

4 GENERATION DESCENDANT GENOGRAM

YOU   **YOUR SPOUSE**

YOUR CHILDREN

THEIR SPOUSES

THEIR CHILDREN
(Draw lines connecting children to their parents.)

CHART OF SYMBOLS FOR GENOGRAM

Simplicity is the key to creating a genogram with notations that will help you identify generational repetitions of traits, problems, illnesses, behaviors, and attitudes. The best system for identifying patterns in the generations of your family tree is the one that you feel comfortable using. A genogram chart includes characters and symbols that represent relationships, as well as medical data and other significant information that impacts the family lineage.

Use the abbreviated symbols and codes described here, or create your own system to indicate specific problems of ancestors or living family members. Consider using colored highlighters to distinguish important information. The patterns that emerge will help you focus your prayers for family healing.

Figure 2. Genogram Codes

Gender:
    male
    female
    dead male
    dead female

Relationships:
    married
    separated
    divorced
    living together
    homosexual
    lesbian
    consanguineous

Progeny:
    unborn baby
    miscarriage/stillbirth

    aborted baby
    identical twins:
      male
      female
    fraternal twins:
      male
      female
      male and female
      adopted/foster child
      separated from family

Figure 2. Genogram Codes

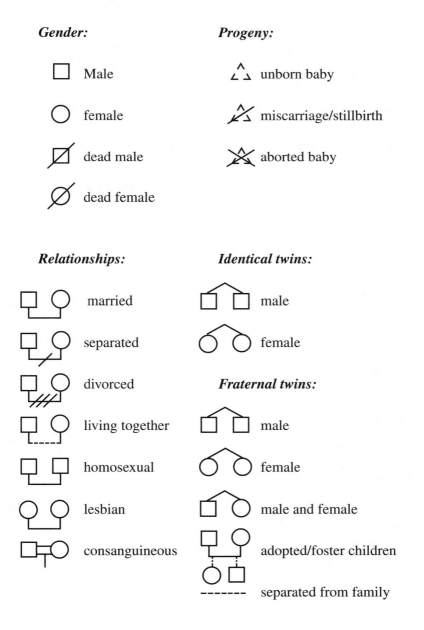

Rooted in Jesus

Genogram Symbols

Abuse:

I	incest
PA	physical abuse
R	rape
SA	sexual abuse
VERB	verbal abuse

Addictions:

ALC	alcholism
DA	drug addiction
ED	eating disorder
GA	gambling addiction
SA	sexual addiction
WA	work addiction
ED	eating disorder

Behavior Disorders:

≶	anger, rage
CO-D	co-dependent
●╴╴╯	criminal
EGO	egocentricity
௸	mental confusion
PTS	post traumatic stress

Beliefs:

†	faith
✝	broken faith
†?	faith unknown

Disability:

DEV	developmental
PHYS	physical
MI	mental illness

Diseases:

AIDS	acquired immune deficiency
ALZ	Alzheimer's disease
AR	arthritis
AS	asthma
CA	cancer
CP	cerebral palsy
EAR	hearing loss
HD	heart disease
MD	muscular dystrophy
MS	multiple sclerosis
PD	Parkinson's
TB	tuberculosis
VIS	vision

Violent Death:

ACC	accident
SU	suicide
V	violent death War:
MIA	missing in action
POW	prisoner of war

APPENDIX II. BRANCHING OUT

As you become acquainted with your ancestors, you may desire to learn more about past generations of your family. Begin with an orderly system for data compilation, and avoid duplication of your research efforts. Some Internet sites and books include printed forms to help you organize census data, vital statistics, and other records.

LIBRARIES AND ARCHIVES

Genealogy libraries are staffed by knowledgeable experts who can guide your search. They may have access to resources that are unknown to you. State archives are resources for records of births, marriages, deaths, plat maps, and other documents. Journals published by local historical societies can broaden your insights into life in the time of your ancestor, even though they may not contain the precise information you need. With persistent digging, you might find your ancestor mentioned in the pages of journals or in cumulative genealogical publications.

The Church of Jesus Christ of the Latter Day Saints (also known as LDS or Mormon) maintains vast compilations of genealogical holdings at the Family History Library in Salt Lake City, Utah. The Mormon Church also operates 3400 family history centers throughout the United States and in 65 foreign countries.

In their desire to baptize all of their ancestors, members have traveled the world to film and compile vital records. For a small fee, you can order microfilms of census and church records, and other valuable data to view on site at a family history center near you. They also maintain a family history database with contributions by church members and others. Because some of the data is undocumented, it may be subject to error. For the nearest Family History Center in the United States, call 1-800-346-6044. (**www.familysearch.org**)

THE NATIONAL ARCHIVES

The National Archives in Washington, D.C., is a repository for four billion records that are useful for genealogical research. The types of information available include: census records, passenger and immigration records, naturalization records, mortality schedules, Freedmen's Bureau records, and others. Many of these records are also available at the National Archives regional branches throughout the United States. A complete listing of records and center locations, along with online help sites, is available at the Web site. (**www.nara.gov**)

THE WORLD WIDE WEB

The Internet has opened up new and expedient paths to genealogy data for those seeking family information. Access to many sites is free, though some require a payment or subscription fee. Since 1997, an online databank has been under construction with indexes to census, passenger arrivals, immigration, naturalization, military service, obituaries, links to surnames, and other historical records. (**www.gensource.com**)

Worldwide, genealogists and volunteers are transferring archival genealogical data into databases that can be accessed by home computers. The immense program is not finished but an enormous amount of data from various countries is already available on the Web. Access the U.S. GenWeb project at **www.genweb.com.** Links to databases of other countries are available at **www.rootsweb.com.**

Cyndi's List, with links to over 63,000 cross-referenced and cross-indexed research sites continues to grow. (**www.cyndislist.com**) Valuable links and free downloadable forms are available at another site. (**www.ancestrycorner.com**)

The Internet is in a constant state of flux, with new sites being developed. They are easy to locate but can seem overwhelming to a novice. A simple way to begin with your browser is to start with the keyword "genealogy." Most sites are user-friendly and provide links to other sites. You will quickly become skilled at navigating the vast number of genealogy sites available. When you find relevant data, you can either print it or save it for future study as a "plain text" document in your word processing program.

Extensive listings of Internet sites for family history research are published in *Everton's Genealogical Helper*, a bimonthly periodical featuring informative articles about research, personal advertisements, and news of genealogy workshops. It is also a source for locating genealogical data on CD-ROMs, record-keeping forms, and professional genealogists. Subjects, localities, and surnames mentioned in each issue are indexed. (**www.everton.com**)

The Ellis Island Immigration Museum honors millions of immigrants who entered America there. The American Immigrant Wall of Honor features plaques inscribed with the names of more than 500,000 individuals and families. At the Foundation's web site, you can view the Wall and obtain information about donating a plaque. (The Statue of Liberty-Ellis Island Foundation, Inc., 52 Vanderbilt Ave., New York, NY 10017-3898 or **www.ellisisland.org**)

Family reunions offer occasions to celebrate kinship. Families unable to gather physically can share frequent electronic reunions. One common and secure Web site provides private family chat rooms for posting pictures and family news. (**www.myfamily.com**)

BOOKS

Your library or bookstore is a resource for genealogy books, as well as comprehensive books and videos generated by the Millennium to describe life and history in the 1900s.

Carmack, Sharon DeBartolo, *Organizing Your Family History Search: Efficient and Effective Ways to Gather and Protect Your Genealogical Research*. OH: Betterway Books, 1999.

Croom, Emily, *The Genealogist's Companion & Sourcebook*. Cincinnati, OH: Betterway Books, 1994. (Reference guide to archival holdings; includes chapters on researching African-American and

Native American genealogy; has some blank forms for organizing research information.)

Crowe, Elizabeth Powell, *Genealogy Online: Researching Your Roots.* NY, SF, Washington, D.C., McGraw-Hill, 1996.

Everton's Genealogical Helper. Everton Publishers, Inc., P.O. Box 368, Logan, UT 84323-0368. Phone: (435) 752-6022.

Gormley, Myra Vanderpool, *Family Diseases: Are You At Risk?* MD: Genealogical Publishing Co., 1989.

Hampsch, John H., C.M.F., *Healing Your Family Tree.* Santa Barbara, CA: Queenship Publishing Co. Books, tapes, and publications: Claretian Tape Ministry, P.O. Box 19100, Los Angeles, CA 90019-0100. **www.claretiantapeministry.org** or (323) 734-1234.

Linn, Matthew, S.J., Linn, Dennis, S.J., and Fabricant, Sheila, *Healing the Greatest Hurt.* NY/Mahwah, NJ: Paulist Press, 1985.

McAll, Dr. Kenneth, *A Guide to Healing the Family Tree.* Santa Barbara, CA: Queenship Publishing Co., 1996.

McAll, Dr. Kenneth, *Healing The Family Tree.* London: Sheldon Press, 1984

Wolfman, Ira, *Do People Grow on Family Trees?: Genealogy for Kids and Other Beginners.* NY: Workman Publishing, 1991.

DOCUMENTARIES

Modern media can transport you through time and allow you to vicariously experience the different eras and circumstances in which your ancestors lived. Some television channels offer educational programs and documentaries and many of these are also available on videos. The wide range of video subjects includes: wars, mental illness, slavery in the South, the Industrial Revolution, the Great Depression, parenting issues, children's behavior, learning disabilities, divorce-related problems, the 1918 influenza epidemic, women's suffrage, and travelogues.

Battlefield Vietnam The war that divided America.

Centennial Events in the West that shaped America.

Hawaii's Last Queen Liliuokalani surrendered her throne to the United States at gunpoint.

Korean War The first large-scale event of the Cold War.

Not for Ourselves Alone Two suffragettes changed the course of history: Elizabeth Cady Stanton and Susan B. Anthony.

Roots Alex Haley launched a worldwide interest in genealogy.

The Civil War The terrible war that united America.

The Great War World War I influenced the Atomic Age, the Cold War, Communism, and conflicts in the Middle East.

The West The impact made by white settlers, adventurers, and exploiters on Native Americans and the environment.

U.S.-Mexican War Dispute between neighbors escalated into a historically significant war.

World War II with Walter Cronkite The war that affected more than three-quarters of the world's population.

(PBS Home Video Catalog, 1-800-645-4727; **www.pbs.org/shop**).

FILMS

Movies that honestly depict historical events and situations that are relevant to family healing provide another way to revisit the past. While many films strive to give a fairly accurate representation of life in the past, keep in mind that writers often take artistic liberties with the events they portray.

ABUSE:

Radio Flyer; The Color Purple

CAPITAL PUNISHMENT:

Dead Man Walking

DISASTERS:

The Grapes of Wrath; The Titanic

FAMILY SECRETS:

The Bridges of Madison County

LABOR UNIONS:

Hoffa; Norma Jean; On the Waterfront

MENTAL ILLNESS:

I Never Promised You a Rose Garden; The Snake Pit.

MULTICULTURAL:

Amistad; Gone With The Wind; In the Name of the Father; Life is Wonderful; Michael Collins; Paradise Road; Roots; Schindler's List; The Diary of Anne Frank; The Field; The Joy Luck Club; The Last Emperor

SURVIVAL:

Paradise Road

WAR:

Bridge on the River Kwai; From Here to Eternity; North and South; Patton; Saving Private Ryan; Sergeant York; The Winds of War; Tora Tora Tora; War and Remembrance.

-The End-